"WE'RE RIGHT and THEY'RE WRONG!"

A COMMON
CHURCH DISEASE

To: Pastor Carolyn J. Lane, Ph.D.

Pray that God uses you
for a long, long time to
bless people.

"WE'RE RIGHT and THEY'RE WRONG!"

A COMMON
CHURCH DISEASE

ANTHONY EDMONDSON

All Old and New Testament quotations are taken from the King James Bible, while all interpretations and expressions are solely from the author.

To order additional copies of this book, contact:
Xlibris Corporation
1-888-795-4274
www.Xlibris.com
Orders@Xlibris.com
77886

Contents

Introduction

To all mature Christians and new converts, a sincere apology is rendered for any misunderstanding concerning the collaboration and interpretation of the Holy Scriptures in order to reach the views expressed in this material. I realize that some conclusions may be difficult for seasoned Christians to accept, and that a freshman disciple may also find them somewhat challenging. Nevertheless, like any epidemic that spreads detrimental consequences into a home, community or nation; the question of where the disease originated, what are its effects, and how it can be cured will always determine the lifespan of its existence. One mission of my book is to discuss several topics that have divided many believers who worship the same God of Abraham, Isaac and Jacob, who profess Jesus Christ as the Son of God, and who accept the Holy Bible to be God's living and written word. Unfortunately, having all these characteristics in common does not create unity. Somewhere the road forks, drawing a line in the sand that not only divides us, but also exalts one group and condemns another. The other mission of my book is to level the playing ground on theology so the scales are not tilted.

As a Christian who used to be a member of the 'Baptist' affiliation for over 20 years, and nurtured by my 12-year 'Methodist' preacher/ stepfather, but now attends a 'Church of Christ'—I can say I've lived diversity firsthand. The experience allowed me to witness churches denouncing churches, preachers slandering preachers, and Christians judging Christians in the attempt to prove "who's right" and "who's wrong." I even conducted a citywide survey with different church affiliations in order to unveil doctrines that had irritated them in the past about each other.

As Christians, when teaching the lost, we do a very good job of staying focused on what matters mostly for them (**salvation**). But when Christians teach other Christians, our agenda to teach what matters mostly for us now (**love**), usually gets substituted by more opinionated, superficial, and diverse concerns. This religious quest for churches to prove *"doctrinal accuracy"* has cost believers enormous interest on their talents before facing the one True Judge. Some Christians live like they really expect the chance to say, "I told you so" to other saints once we get to heaven.

While we don't have to eliminate the 'trying of the spirit' or embrace another belief over our own, we do need to ask ourselves how much more effective would Christians be if we spread the Gospel as a unit, rather than opposing groups. How much time have we wasted on judging and debating with another Christian, when we should've been seeking a lost soul or desperately turning the backslider around?

Hopefully, after reading this book your knowledge, purpose, and attitude will be better prepared to help you discern what not to waste precious time on, along with having understood more spiritual mysteries, as you rid yourself of a disease that continues to contaminate the body of Christ.

May the God of heaven and earth open your understanding to the fullest.

Bias and Prejudice Materials Used in Bible Study

When was the first book written to accompany the Bible? What do you think inspired the author to sense the need to assist the Bible in some of its teachings? Like you, I'm not sure either. But it's clear that today there are millions of books out there claiming to walk hand-in-hand with it. In fact, if you go online in search of Christian books and magazines, you would sink into an atmosphere similar to a pet shop flooded with Bible literature barking "pick me," "pick me!" (*Ecc. 12:12 ". . . of making many books there is no end . . ."*) But unlike a wagging tail on the cute puppy that temporally appeases our companionship, not choosing the right 'study book' for Bible topics will have serious consequences. Because receiving the 'wrong doctrine' means supporting the 'wrong church,' and supporting the 'wrong church' means 'find-another-one' in our society.

Not surprisingly, most preachers, elders and teachers collect their study materials based on 'in-house' recommendations. There's nothing wrong with this—just make sure you're aware that the suggested materials are usually tailored around the interpretation and belief of its affiliation. Thus, if this is the only kind of literature used in search of doctrinal truths, it could greatly limit your resources and promote ignorance as well. (*Mark 12:24 ". . . do you not therefore error because you know not the scriptures . . ." Hosea: 4:6 "My people are destroyed for lack of knowledge . . ." Proverbs 18:17: "He that is first in his own cause seemeth just . . ." Proverbs 14:12 "There is a way that seemeth right unto man, but the end therefore are the ways of death." Proverbs 28:26 "He that trusteth in his own heart is a fool . . ."*)

All through the Bible and on today's political pages we can read wherever choice or advice is available, counsellorship will represent itself with more than one opinion. (*Proverbs 11:14 ". . . but in the multitude of counsellors there is safety"*) Imagine our judicial system coming to its conclusion based on one testimony. If there's going to be a thorough investigation of doctrinal truths, one has to weigh-in on views other than its own. Another scenario that causes error is we sometimes settle too quickly for a good answer rather than wait for the best one. How many times have we craved a second opportunity to re-do something, because we later discover that a better way was hidden in the rough? This is what will often happen if we only use one eye and one ear. To mandate study materials under any other guideline could breed discrimination, propaganda, and ideology.

Still, examining other views may sound like a simple way of solving the problem, but grafting even a phrase of another 'belief' where opposing doctrine is taught could be 'membership catastrophe.' Besides, don't we all teach what we believe?—for no man teaches what he does not believe. So what are you going to do, continue being taught one doctrine by one affiliation?

Yes and No. You're going to pray harder and start asking the instructor more questions. Request scriptural passages that command Christians word-for-word, or by example. If a teacher uses the term "I believe" or "I think" as their strongest defense, ask them to show you in the Bible how they came to that conclusion. And don't quit asking questions just because they've shown confidence in their answer. Continue to ask questions until you are enlightened.

While it's true that some topics will require more time to study than your regular session allows, make sure you continue the acquisition until your understanding is fine-tuned. Sadly, some inquiries will end in disagreement, but at least you've created a habit of tracking the truth as well as knowing it. Please remember to present yourself at all times as a Christian, not confusing the listeners with vain opinions and arguments. (*2 Timothy 2:16 "Keep away from profane and foolish discussions, which only drive people further away from God." Ephesians 4:29 "Let no corrupt communication proceed out of your mouth, but that which is good to the use of edifying" 2 Timothy 2:14 ". . . charging them before the Lord that they strive not with words to no profit.")*

++ As volunteered members of your local congregation, you are expected to support your church institution through finance, prayers, deeds and attendance. You are also responsible for honoring church protocol concerning worship days, songs, offerings, business meetings, sermons, seminars, dress codes and assignments. But you are not obligated to accept at face value any teachings outside of the Bible as doctrinal truth without challenge or burden-of-proof. This attitude to produce factual documents concerning the gospel began with the early Christians: (*Acts 17:11 ". . . . in that they received the word with all readiness of mind, and searched the scriptures daily, whether those things are so"*).

Must a Person be Baptized to be Saved

This controversial topic has been around almost as long as the church itself. It looks like as soon as the dust settled over the *Gentiles* being recognized as God's people by the *Jews*, baptism became the next debate on the church roster. Matter of fact, this subject may even play a major role in the purchasing of my book. I imagine most potential readers will scroll the contents and then fan through the pages directly to this topic. Proclaiming or disclaiming baptism to be essential to salvation is normally the jewel that credits your entire doctrinal worthiness for many Christians.

To begin, let's review several scriptural passages that advocate baptism as part of salvation. (*1 Peter 3:20-21 ". . . . wherein few that is, eight souls were saved by water" . . . "The like figure whereunto even baptized doth also now save us . . ." Mark 16:16 "He that believeth and is baptized . . ." Luke 3:7 ". . . multitude came to be baptized . . ." John 1:33 ". . . he that sent me to baptize . . ." Acts 2:38 ". . . repent and be baptized . . ." 2:41 ". . . gladly received word were baptized . . ." 8:36 ". . . what does hinder me to be baptized" 18:8 ". . . many believed and were baptized" 22:16 ". . . be baptized and wash away thy sins . . ." 1 Corinthians 12:13 ". . . all baptized into one body . . ." Matt. 3:6 "And were baptized of him in Jordan, confessing their sins."*)

The above passages are only a few that teach baptism by word or example. But with scriptures so apparent, how could doubt, confusion and debate climb into the pulpit and separate so many of us?

A lot of Christians utilize and rely mainly on the situation surrounding the 'thief on the cross' as argument to disclaim baptism. (*Luke 23:43* "*. . . 'Verily I say unto thee, today shalt thou be with me in paradise.'*") Although that was an isolated case, it is true that many passages in the New Testament Bible do not include, or necessarily suggest, baptism to be required as the completion of salvation. (*Romans 10:9 "That if thou shalt confess with thou mouth the Lord Jesus, and shalt believe in thine heart that God has raised him from dead, thou shalt be saved" Galatians 3:11 ". . . the just shall live by faith" John 3:16 "For God so loved the world, that he gave his only begotten Son, that whosoever believeth in him should not perish, but have everlasting life" Romans 4:5 "But to him that worketh not, but believeth on him that justifieth the ungodly, his faith is counted for righteous" Romans 3:28 "Therefore we conclude that a man is justified by faith without the deeds of the law" Romans 5:9 "Much more then, being now justified by his blood, we shall be saved from wrath through him."*)

Even the mass at one time asked Jesus the question of what does it take to do the will of God: (*John 6:28 "Then said they unto him, What shall we do, that we might work the works of God?" 6:29 "Jesus answered and said unto them, 'This is the work of God, that ye believe on him whom he sent' "*). This understanding through these passages has resulted in Christians dismissing the activity of baptism altogether or indulging in it for means other than salvation.

Where does it all fit together, and where does it all fall apart? Interpretation, teachings, trust, belief, and hardness of the heart are the blame for most of it. *Matt. 3:1-15* reveals that people were being baptized for the remission of sins before Jesus was baptized, during Jesus' ministry, and after his death as well. It started before Jesus' death and continued after his resurrection. Jesus also commands the disciples while he ascends toward heaven to baptize people. (*Matt. 28:19 "Go ye therefore, and teach all nations, baptizing them in the name of the Father, and of the Son, and the Holy Ghost."*)

God's divine word in the Bible is not confusing. What causes misunderstandings and quarrels over what's correct and incorrect concerning the Bible arises predominately because the majority of churchgoers depend on their mentors. Lots of wealthy people place immense trust in their accountant to make educated and loyal decisions with their valuables. As a result of their excessive confidence in the accountant, IRS tax violations may leave them with no margin to defend themselves during audits.

Likewise, many Christians are caught off-guard when approached with doctrine that contradict what they believe about *Baptism* and are left only with what others have taught them. Paul warns us about not being prepared to answer questions on our own. (*1 Peter 3:15 ". . . . ready always to give every man that asketh a reason for the hope that is in you . . ."*) Countless Christian brothers and sisters have spoken quite foolishly because of what someone else has persuaded them to be truthful, without ever really examining for themselves if their belief complies totally with the Gospel. And even when many of us discover we're wrong, very few will welcome the correction or extend a later apology to the challenger.

++ I am convinced that no Christian wants to be turned away from heaven because he wasn't emerged in water. Water is not strange to believers, especially to us Floridians. We drink it, bathe in it, and clean with it. Plus, we spend 75% of our lives near a swimming pool or on the beach. And I'm sure within a few days you're going to come near it again. So rather than delay or debate a simple action that many say will decide our eternity, why not let everyone of us enjoy one more splash for a divine reason all in the name of the *Father, Son,* and the *Holy Ghost?*

Can Musical Instruments Be a Part of Worship Service

This is another topic that causes Christians to point their eyebrows down at each other. I heard one talk show guest say, "I am a true worshipper of the Most High, and the playing of instruments or not doesn't decide if God gets my praise and worship. 'Cause if I'm really sincere about worshipping the Lord, I'll let nothing stop me." I thought that was an eye-opener.

No matter how revealing the quote was, I know you still want scriptural passages that support one's belief either way. One reason why the majority of churches choose and are comfortable with the playing of instruments during worship services, is because it was permitted amongst God's people in the Old Testament. (*2 Chronicles. 7:3 "And when all the children of Israel saw how fire came down, and the glory of the Lord upon the house, they bowed their faces to the ground upon the pavement, and worshipped, and praised the Lord . . ." 5:12 "Also the Levites which were the singers, all of them of Asaph, of Heman, of Jeduthun, with their sons and their brethren, being arrayed in white linen, having cymbals and psalteries and harps, stood at the east end of the alter . . ."*)

We also read in the book of Revelation that *John* heard and saw musical instruments being used as a part of worship in heaven (*Rev. 14:2 ". . . . and I heard the voice of harpers harping with their harps" 14:3 "And they sung as it were a new song before the throne . . ." 5:8 "the four beast and four and twenty elders fell down before the Lamb, having everyone of them harps . . ."*), and there are more passages in the 'Old Testament' and in 'Revelation' that rule instruments acceptable during worship.

But what about another scriptural passage that many Christians believe condemns the usage of musical instruments during worship services and tolerates no part of it? (*Ephesians 5:19 "Speaking to yourselves in psalms and hymns and spiritual songs, singing and making melody in your heart to the Lord."*) They insist that the above passage identifies psalms and hymns and spiritual songs as authorized by God. It further provides a direct statement or command that the only instrument which can make melody in our heart is our voice. There also is the belief that these songs' agendas were to teach and admonish one another, rather than to sound pleasing to the ear. They were not for emotional enjoyment, but for edification. Many non-denominational worshippers agree that God does not approve or authorize musical instruments for the New Testament church, because they find no direct statement, apostolic example, or necessary inference (scriptural reasons) that gives them other interpretations. And if a church does include musical instruments during worship; on what Godly authority does it have to display this kind of practice.

This is the only subject in the Bible where Christians make God look like he doesn't know what he wants. First we see he allowed music in the past and disallows it in the present, but then re-allows it again once believers get to heaven. We cannot deny that there aren't numerous passages in the Bible that point to the usage of lyres, tambourines, harps, cymbals and trumpets during the worshipping of God. But what mainly contributes to conflict in doctrine is *'Ephesians 5:19'* and *'Colossians 3:16'*.

Before interpreting *'Ephesians 5:19'* as a commandment that rules musical instruments NOT being allowed during worship service, let's research a few surrounding passages that helps keep the verse in its context. If any person will read all of *Ephesians Chapter 5* or the entire *Ephesians Book*, one will quickly understand that *Paul* is talking about the old way we walked, and the new way we should walk once becoming Christians. When *Paul* informed the Ephesians to speak hymns, psalms and spiritual songs to each other, and make melody in their hearts unto the Lord, he knew this wasn't a new commandment or new way to worship the Lord, or a suggestion to get rid of music instruments. In fact, this commandment, *Ephesians 5:19*, sprouted from an old commandment in (*Deuteronomy 11:19-20 "And ye shall teach them, your children, speaking of them when thou sittest in thine house, and when thou walkest by the way, and when thou liest down, and when thou riseth up. And thou shall write them upon the door posts of thy house and upon thy gates").* What was the purpose of constantly teaching the children to memorize the acts and ways of the Lord outside of the Temple? The same reasons we are to speak to ourselves in psalms and hymns and spiritual songs today: to remain familiar with God, his accomplishments, and our faith. *Paul's* emphasis and concern in this epistle was not focusing on what Christians did in worship service, but how they carried themselves outside the synagogue in their daily walk. The behaviors that *Paul* is writing about in the latter verses of *Ephesians Chapter 4*, the entire *Ephesians Chapter 5*, and the first half of *Ephesians Chapter 6* are pertaining to how we carry ourselves in our social lives, not during church worship. The bad behaviors that *Paul* is referring to usually occurs during our social encounters, not during worship or church visits. (*Ephesians 5:15 "See then that you walk circumspectly, not as fools, but as wise" 5:2 "And walk in love . . ." 5:8 "For ye were sometimes darkness, but now are ye light in the Lord: walk as children of light."*) Also, if you read in *Ephesians Chapter 5* and exclude verse *19*, most of these behaviors do replicate worldly activities. What do you think *Paul* is talking about in *Ephesians 5:11-12 (". . . . but rather reprove them" "For it is a shame even to speak of those things which are done of them in secret")*. Where did these activities commonly and mainly manifest, in their social lives or at church? *Paul* even continues through *Chapter 6* about how we should conduct ourselves with our spouses, our children, our employees and with the ones in authority. These instructions and behaviors are not of church matters, but of social indulgencies. *Ephesians 4:29* will also help explain and keep *Ephesians 5:19* within its context. Likewise, *Colossians 3:8-9* helps explain *Colossians 3:16*, shedding more light towards the needed mannerism in a Christian's social life (*Col. 3:18-22*). *Paul* knew in a close-knit society Christians encountered Christians in market places, during recreation, on basic journeys, and on their jobs without possessing music instruments or sacred scrolls. *Ephesians 5:19* is a verse that commands us to be pleasant and loving in our communication; instructing that we should speak words that lift up and encourage through the examples of the lyrics in hymns, spiritual songs, and psalms while keeping the Lord primary in our hearts as we meditate on his word. This is one way believers of that era were going to remain inspired and familiar with the scriptures. Plus in *Paul's* letter to the *'Colossians'* he includes *'Ephesians 5:19'* again to help persuade

Christians to put off the 'old man' they used to walk in. (*Colossians 3:7 "In the which ye also walked sometime, when you lived in them" 3:1 "If ye then be risen with Christ, seek those things which are above . . ."*) *Paul* does not use the term "in their worship," but "in their walk," which clearly means he is referring to a Christian's behavior in society, not in worship service. Even when Christians who worship God with musical instruments point out Bible verses, where *John* wrote about instruments being used in heaven around God's throne, *Rev. 14:2-3,* Christians who still disagree believe, "What is happening or will happen in heaven is not a pattern for New Testament worship." But if that statement is true, then it must be a biblical error in *Matt. 16:19 ". . . and whatsoever thou shalt loose on earth shall be loosed in heaven"* (Jesus to Peter). And if people want to continue their campaign of worship practices in heaven does not pertain to New Testament worship, then this would imply that Jesus made a huge mistake in the Lord's Prayer: *Matt. 6:10 "Thy kingdom come, Thy will be done in earth as it is in heaven."* Not only is Jesus supporting the way God is being worshipped in heaven, but he is teaching us to pray as well that the same wills in heaven be applied and fulfilled on earth, and one will does include a particular worship practice that allows musical instruments. These are scriptures that openly suggest some heavenly and earthly practices to be integrated. But still there may be one final arrow shot to disclaim any of the above instrumental privileges, and that is: "On what authority" does a Christian have to discern *Ephesians 5:19* any other way except for to NOT play musical instruments during worship service? The authority would be based on their faith. *(Romans 5:1 ". . . being justified by faith . . .")* The book of *Hebrews* has many passages on authority, or actions, justified through faith. It tells all of us, *"But without faith it is impossible to please God." Hebrews 13:5 "Examine yourselves, whether ye be in faith, prove your own selves . . ."* Jesus informs us that what we believe or speak is what we will be judged by *(Matt. 12:37 "For by your words thou shalt be justified, and by thy words you shalt be condemned" Matt. 12:34 . . . out of the abundance of the heart the mouth speaks).* All of these actions have something to do with one's faith.

Musical Instruments has been a part of worship to God by his children and has never been denounced by commandment. Only through the misinterpretation of those who have taken a single passage out of context and chose to implement it as scriptural requirement does it have merit.

++ Nowhere do we read in *'Ephesians 5'* that *Paul* is commanding us to keep order in church service through the withdrawing of musical instruments. Yes, *Paul* does instruct us intensely concerning harmony and church protocol during worship meetings in the book of *'Corinthians'* and in the book of *'Timothy'*. But I find no scriptures prohibiting musical instruments in the Bible. Everyone who studies the Bible knows that it is ill-advised, selfish, and dangerous to take a single passage and conclude a paragraph, chapter, or book. And unfortunately, this is what might have happened to all who condemn others who DO take pleasure and confidence in worshipping God with musical instruments. If we read *Romans Chapter 14* and understand that everyone is not convicted by someone else's faith, then this may subside or relieve the responsibility of condemning others who do not agree in Bible doctrine or theology.

The only direct guideline in which a Christian is instructed to worship the Father is with his inner being, and in the most pure, honest manner (*John 4:23 "But the hour cometh, and now is, when true worshippers shall worship the Father in spirit and in truth" 4:23 "God is Spirit: and they that worship him must worship him in spirit and in truth"*), and that those who worship God must believe he exists, and that he rewards the ones who seek him sincerely and constantly. (*Hebrews 11:6 "... for he that cometh to God must believe that he is, and that he is a rewarder of them that diligently seek him."*) Again, help cure the disease that causes churches to resist fellowship with one another. (*Romans 14:22 "Hast thou faith? have it to thyself before God. Happy is he that condemneth not himself in that thing which he alloweth."*)

Weddings, Funerals and Other Activities on Church Grounds

Although this topic doesn't receive as much attention as the previous ones, it still measures to be a dividing factor when witnessed by opposing Christians. No matter how romantic the weddings are, how sympathetic the funeral may be, or how important the cause represents—these events are not welcomed on some church grounds.

Let's start first with activities practiced on 'sacred grounds' during the days of Moses when the Israelites came to worship God. (*Deut. 12:7 "And there you shall eat before the Lord your God, and you shall rejoice in all that he put in your hand unto . . ." 14:26 ". . . and thou shalt eat there before the Lord thy God, and thou shalt rejoice, thou, and thine household."*) Also during the 'Dedication of the Temple', Solomon consecrated part of the Temple courtyard to make offerings because the bronze alter was too small. (*2 Chronicles 7:7 "Moreover Solomon hallowed the middle of the court that was before the house of the Lord: for there he offered burnt offerings, and the fat of the peace offerings . . ." 7:8 "Also at the same time Solomon kept the feast seven days, and all Israel with him . . ."*)

Not only did the 'Dedication of the Temple' feed hundreds of thousands of people on sacred grounds, but it was a physical endeavor as well. Imagine maintaining all that livestock and preparing those massive sacrifices. Such tactics had to require a commercial process equivalent to every Super Bowl tailgate party combined.

But, some will say, "That was a part of the Old Testament, not the New Testament."

Well, Jesus' first miracle was recorded in the book of *John* when he turned the water into wine at a **wedding**. (*John 2:9 "When the ruler of the feast had tasted the water that was made wine . . ."*)

Although this marriage ceremony wasn't on 'sacred grounds,' the occasion symbolizes and represents what most people, even Christians, have sadly overlooked.

This explanation will have nothing to do with flower arrangements, four-tier cakes, and packed assembles—it's more prophetic than that. (1) At a wedding you witness a relationship that's committed by understandable and agreeable vows. (2) The only circumstance that can legally separate the married party is unfaithfulness or death. (3) The bride and groom look forward to being together as long as time permits them because they love each other very much.

Is it not ironic that Jesus chose to attend a wedding before healing the blind, curing the diseased, and feeding the hungry? He knew, even though death would've ridded the people of those trials, it couldn't have ever painted the real picture of him preparing a place and returning as the *groom* to marry the *church*, his bride. Look at all the personalities a bride and groom symbolize together—unity, joy, security, respect, loyalty, peace, trust, love.

God used Adam and Eve as primary examples of how a bride and groom mirrored the future of Christ and the Church. Plus, Jesus used illustrations of a bride and groom throughout his ministry. Even the story of *Joseph* and *Mary* plays a significant role in terms of what happens when the groom discovers his bride is unfaithful. All of it goes hand-in-hand, and maybe that's why church weddings are more tolerated than frowned upon. *Paul* sums it up with this confession: (*1 Corinthians 15:19 "If in this life only we have hope in Christ, we are of all men most miserable"*) Marriage between two Christians helps to remind us that the Lord is coming back to claim and unite with his loved ones.

21

Funerals held in church buildings are also common. I do not know where the custom originated, but examining how it might have come into existence is far less exhausting. Even though my stepfather was a preacher and mortician, I neither inquired nor was told why most funerals were showcased inside church buildings.

It relates to the question of how man began to cook his food instead of eating it raw. Some say he was warming his hands while eating meat and accidentally dropped it into the fire, and while he was seeking a way to retrieve the meat, it had partially cooked. One bite and the rest was history. Another theory includes the story of our ancestors entering a burned forest, came across some of the cooked animals, and had no choice but to eat them. Again—one bite and the rest was history. (No, I'm not advocating evolution.) How we decided to cook our food is no longer relevant today—we just want it done.

In a similar manner, unless there is proof, we can only assume the first church funeral had to be in honor of a devout, religious figure—a longtime, highly-respected preacher or pastor. Someone who may have held the highest position in the assembly. Perhaps this person was so well-liked that no other place would accommodate or signify what *John Doe* was best known or appreciated for. Next thing you know, another religious or political figure receives the royal treatment also. Finally, Romeo and Juliet, the king's two wives, the boy next door, and the mailman all qualify for a church funeral wherever permitted.

Are there biblical recordings of funerals? Sort of. While deaths and burials of *Jesus, Abraham, Joseph, David, Solomon, Samuel,* and *John the Baptist* are mentioned, the only types of funeral services I recognize to be considered as recorded funerals are the ones held inside the homes of the deceased's loved ones. Today, where funerals are granted will depend mainly on country, culture, era, and laws. While most of the ancient world did not identify their worship centers as churches, many of the nations built synagogues that were equal in purpose. Paul used these landmark structural assembles as his platforms to spread the Gospel. (*Acts 17:2 "And Paul as his manner was, went in unto them . . ."*)

Although I find no Bible verses that allow or the disallow funerals to be permitted inside church buildings, there is a passage that commands

Christians to honor God's place of worship. (*Leviticus 19:30 ". . . and reverence my sanctuary: I am the Lord."*) Also, God expresses how he feels about our treating what belongs to him as ordinary. (*Leviticus 19:8 "Therefore everyone that eateth it shall bear his iniquity, because he hath profaned the hallowed thing of the Lord . . ."*) And King Belshazzar was condemned because he used Temple dishes during his banquet. (*Daniel 5:22-23 ". . . Belshazzar hast not humbled thine heart, though thou knewest all this, but hast lifted up thyself against the Lord of heaven: and they have brought the vessels of his house before thee, and thou, and thy lords, thy wives, and thy concubines, have drunk wine in them, and has praised the gods of gold, silver, brass, iron and wood . . ."*)

There's also the issue of church grounds being used for **other social activities** to enhance financial stability, all in the name of the Gospel: car washes, bake-offs, yard sales and dinners. Does the church have authority? Do these events help spread the Gospel as much as they claim? Can this publicized invitation keep its participants out of heaven?

If we examine this case as though it were in today's courtroom, the prosecutor might ask the defendant, "Is there money deposited in the 'John Doe Church' account without the above activities having a role?" The defendant would have to say, "Yes, we take up a collection during worship service." Then the prosecutor would ask his next question: "Are there any foods and beverages consumed during or after worship service on sacred grounds?" The defendant would truthfully answer, "Yes, bread and wine during Communion." The prosecutor would then ask, "Are there any children who eat snacks, or anybody who eat breath mints?" "Do the mothers leave the grounds when they feed their babies?" "Does anybody every finish an egg sandwich in the car on sacred grounds?" And then the defendant would hesitantly reply, "Well, yeah, no—I guess, but that's different!" That's when the prosecutor would face the jury and say, "This proves that the defendant has no legal rights, since 'John Doe Church' is guilty of implementing the use of money and food on sacred grounds as well." See how crazy things can get when we play 'watchdog' against another church, preacher, or Christian?

++ I know religion can sometimes get a little "don't do this and don't do that." But as much as this may bother a lot of people, many religious teachings won't be resolved until the end of time. (*1 Corinthians 3:13*

"Every man's work shall be made manifest: for the day shall declare it, because it shall be revealed by fire; and the fire shall try every man's work of what sort it is" 3:14 "If any man's work abide which he hath built thereupon, he shall receive a reward" 3:15 "If any man's work shall be burned, he shall suffer loss: but he himself shall be saved; yet so as by fire".) This conclusive judgment is also supported by Jesus in another scripture: (*Matt. 5:19 "Whoever therefore shall break one of these least commandments, and shall teach men so, he shall be called the least in the kingdom of heaven . . ."*). Neither scripture implies that an individual will be cast into hell because his theology is incorrect. Although it is clear that he will lose a reward in heaven of significant value.

Marriage, Divorce, and Unlawful Marriage

This topic divides church affiliations wider than the Red Sea did at the time of Moses and the children of Israel crossing it. It's the most sensitive, convicting, liberating subject a married, divorced, or remarried couple can be instructed on. If you considered casting my book into the garbage because of its earlier chapters, some interpretations during this discussion will probably be the virus that shuts down your computer.

Before targeting scriptural passages that forbid or permit, allow or disallow, condemn or pardon in this matter, we'll have to consider God's plan and intention of marriage. We'll also have to discuss God's attitude about divorce, and what constitutes an unlawful marriage along with its problems and resolutions.

We read in the book of '*Genesis*' that God created the earth and gave instructions to all living creatures by the sixth day and then rested on the seventh day: (*Genesis 2:2 "And on the seventh day God ended his work which he had made; and he rested on the seventh day from all his work which he made." Genesis 1:27 "So God created man in his own image . . .").*

Then after several more verses we read where God's concern and strategy for Adam's companionship is resolved. (*Genesis 2:18 "And the Lord said, 'It is not good that the man should be alone; I will make him a help meet for him'" 2:21 "And the Lord God caused a deep sleep to fall upon Adam, and he slept: and he took one of his ribs, and closed up the flesh instead thereof" 2:22 "And the rib, which the Lord God had taken from man, made he woman, and brought her unto the man" 2:23 "And Adam said, 'This is now bone of my bones, and flesh of my flesh: she shall be called Woman, because she was taken out of Man'" 2:24 "Therefore shall a man leave his father and his mother, and shall cleave unto his wife: and they shall become one flesh." Gen. 1:28 "And God blessed them and God said unto them, 'Be fruitful, and multiply, and replenish the earth, and subdue it . . .")*

Talk about a **marriage** made in heaven that came with a full-proof plan. The verse that quotes God, *"Therefore shall a man leave his father and his mother, and shall cleave unto his wife,"* advocates that he ordained and commanded it to be instituted into every intimate relationship between a man and a woman. Plus, his instruction to multiply, be fruitful, and replenish the earth could happen only through the process of sexual intercourse, and we know God would never instruct people to sin against him.

Now that we've discussed *why marry* and *who orchestrated marriage*, let's see what God's attitude is about divorce and the importance of couples staying together. We read in the book of *'Malachi,'* how God feels about the 'D' word. (*Malachi 2:16 "For the Lord, the God of Israel, saith that he hateth putting away . . ."*) Things can't get any clearer than that expression. One might think, "You mean if I'm being abused by my spouse, lied to, and get very little respect or support, God still commands me to remain married?"

Yep, even if you separate for the reason of safety and peace, you're still expected to remain married under those circumstances. (*Matt. 19:6 "Wherefore they are no more twain, but one flesh. What therefore God has joined together, let no man put asunder."*) Just as in today's society we have legitimate divorce laws, the ancient Jews embraced their legitimate divorce protocol through the law of Moses. (*Matt. 19:7 ". . . why did Moses then command to give a writing of divorcement, and put her away?"*) Not only was Jesus familiar with the Law of Moses, but he knew why it surfaced, and that it was to be used only as an alternative to God's marriage plan. (*Matt. 19:8 ". . . Moses because of the hardness of your hearts suffered you to put away your wives: but from the beginning it was not so."*) The only considerable reason that may possess an inkling of justification for **divorce** would be unfaithfulness. (*Matt. 19:9 "And I say unto you,*

'Whosoever shall divorce his wife, except it be for fornication, and shall marry another, committeth adultery.' ")

The notion that a man had to keep his less-than-honorable wife sounded ludicrous; especially when he had been previously granted the right to divorce her if she got too fat, too old, too nagging, or too anything that cramped his style. Jesus' conviction proved to be overbearing even for his elite twelve. (*Matt. 19:10 "His disciples say unto him, 'If the case of the man be so with his wife, it is not good to marry.' "*)

And there are more scriptural passages that suppress divorce and advocate maintaining the marriage. (*1 Corinthians 7:16 "For what knowest thou, O wife, whether thou shalt save thy husband, or how knowest thou, O man, whether thou shalt save thy wife?" 7:11 "But and if she depart, let her remain unmarried, or be reconciled to her husband: and let not the husband put away his wife."*)

Even though '*1 Corinthians 7:16*' is referring to circumstances involving Christians being married to non-Christians, the emphasis and purpose of the passage is obviously against divorce. The strategy of commanding a couple to either stay single or reconcile with each other is one genius stipulation. Just consider the idea of you being without your spouse means you being without anyone. What kind of weird resolution is that? Billions of people in the world, and everyone is exempt to you but your spouse? How dare God implement a clause like that into your marriage? What was he thinking, right?

The purpose of this plan is to take away 98 of your 100 choices and leave you with only two roads to travel. That in itself will give you a rude awakening. If you have only one person to be intimate with, one person to keep you warm at night, one person to show the world you're not alone, and only one person to spend the rest of your life with, then your efforts to stay together will be a million times greater.

Suddenly the few pounds she gained doesn't look so bad after all. Or that thing you argued three days in a row over wasn't as important as it seemed. Now the choice of watching a football game with the fellows doesn't hold a candle compared to spending time with your wife doing dishes in the kitchen. Watching every episode of Reality TV Court isn't as colorful as watching your husband do a minor repair on the car. The list goes on and on.

My point is that grown-ups are a lot like children in this matter: we get away with whatever we can. God's plan in the above verses constricts, eliminates, and directs us in the right way to go. If we follow his plan of marriage and divorce, we will have no choice but to shed our bratty behaviors and re-evaluate our vows and commitments. We'll become easier to get along with and exhibit much more self control in the war on temptation. That's when all your love will be channeled to the right person in a manner that glorifies God.

Although last, this subject is certainly not the least. What should two people do when they have violated God's laws that govern the authority of divorce and re-marriage? Many, many Christians, then and now, are wrestling with these topics. For the divorced Christian; no matter how self-justified or long ago it happened, every time a sermon is preached about divorce, if biblical passages weren't instituted to dissolve the marriage, a black cloud reminds the poor souls that God has a beef with them.

Even worse, what about the happily married couple who finally accepts a church invitation, only to sit through an hour of ruling their marriage as unlawful. So they leave the assembly fighting a 'wrong marriage' and trying to decide where they're going to get advice from, along with what to do with each other in the meantime.

Nothing is more fearful and frustrating than to be approached with a scripture that endorses condemnation for an act we've committed, especially when there's little, if anything, we can change about it. Most divorced "ex's" are either married to someone else by now or would never consider **remarrying** them again anyway. On the flip side, couples who have married outside of biblical guidelines, who are instructed to separate, face far more difficult decisions. It's not enough that they have a thorn in their wedded side and are advised to abandon the comfort and stability that may have blossomed from a healthy marriage, but they most likely share properties, mutual friends, future goals, and sometimes children.

The next thing we know is they're casting aside helpful and inspiring activities in order to quickly settle the disturbing news they've suddenly absorbed. Because in reality, we are talking about God, us, heaven and hell. As Christians we know the day is coming when we're going to give an account of everything we've done in our bodies. (*Romans 14:10 ". . . for we shall all stand before the judgment seat of Christ" Hebrews 9:27 "And it is appointed unto men once to die, but after this the judgment."*)

Anytime you're facing judgment for breaking a law, there are only one of two ways to conclude the matter. You are either found guilty or innocent, and these are piercing concerns for Christians who are living in an unauthorized divorce or marriage. Before we speed toward the conclusion, let's examine a few passages that elaborate on both subjects.

We learn early from the 'Ten Commandments' that adultery is not permissible (*Exodus 20:14 "Thou shalt not commit adultery"*), and Jesus sheds even more light on the subject of adultery by judging it from the root. (*Matt. 5:28 "But I say unto you, that whosoever looketh on a woman to lust after her hath committed adultery with her already in his heart."*) Being that Jesus was heard saying this by hundreds of listeners during the 'sermon on the mount,' the scribes and Pharisees attempted to trap him with his answer for the penalty of adultery. (*John 8:3 " And the scribes and Pharisees brought unto him a woman taken in adultery . . ." 8:5 "Now Moses in the law commanded us, that such should be stoned: but what sayest thou? "*) Now that we've accepted adultery to be a no-no, let's see how it blames unauthorized divorces and marriages to be solely responsible for the entire problem.

Clearly, the Pharisees weren't satisfied or pleased with Jesus' response to the 'woman caught in adultery', and so indulged in another opportunity to trap him with more illustrations concerning marriage and divorce. (*Matt. 19:3 "The Pharisees also came unto him, tempting him, and saying unto him, 'Is it lawful for a man to divorce his wife for every cause?' "*) Of course Jesus takes the time and explains it from the beginning about God's plan for marriage between a man and woman, how the two become one flesh, and that this is the reason a man leaves his parents and clings to his wife.

Well, the Pharisees already knew this saying, and by anticipating Jesus' quotes from the scriptures, they conceived that they had the perfect question to discredit his teaching. (*Matt. 19:7 "They say unto him, 'Why did Moses then command to give writing of divorcement, and to put her away?'"*) Here is where Jesus exposes all who's involved in adultery when divorce is applied outside of biblical reasoning. (*Matt. 19:9 ". . . except it be for fornication, and shall marry another, committeth adultery, and whosoever marrieth her which is divorced doth commit adultery."*) Even more punishing is the latter part of the conviction: the people who are divorced for being unfaithful carry that adulterous sin to whoever marries them.

So Jesus confirms whoever divorces for the wrong reason is guilty of committing adultery to himself, and is guilty of causing two more people to become guilty if they marry, also. Wow—are you your brother's keeper? Now you're starting to understand the real impact of divorce. Not because it's evidence of a failed, embarrassed and painful marriage, but because you know the seriousness of God's expectation on commitment to Him, and to your spouse.

Unfortunately, this dark side of divorce crosses so far over into remarriages that many preachers of different affiliations will not join a divorced couple in matrimony. They will gladly do the honors with a *first-time couple* or *widower*. But in order to stay on the safe side they will decline any marriage assistance outside of counseling, even if the parties have documents stating them as divorce petitioners.

Still, we know when two people want to marry they are going to find other resources to accommodate them. Whether it's a 'justice of the peace,' notary public, Vegas or another preacher, "*I do*" eventually prevails. But when a second-married couple is pointed out through scripture by peers and mentors that their 'oneness' is a prime candidate for dissolution, the surprising heartache can rapidly lead them to desperate measures of salvaging their proudest moment. Unfortunately, studying with a teacher from the accusing establishment will only lead to more convictions, since they're the ones who called them out in the first place. Like a doctor who concludes you have cancer, your backup plan is to immediately obtain a second opinion before lying on the table.

I am familiar with a newly-wedded couple who experienced a similar situation. Both individuals were previously married, and both individuals were the petitioners in their divorces. Both individuals had circumstantial evidence that unfaithfulness was grafted into their marriages by their spouses, and with one "ex" even married at the time. Although both individuals came from different church affiliations, they professed to be Christians and were willing to worship God together at the congregation that seemed to promote the most spiritual growth.

Week after week the couple attended church service and was gathering spiritual food each sermon. The groom was absolutely flourishing in marriage and in scripture, but the bride developed a conviction in her spirit that tore at the seam of their marriage. Upon her daily Bible study she had ran across *Matthew 19*, and from then on saw herself burning in the pits of hell because she wasn't sure if she divorced her husband of two decades for the right reason. Suddenly the guilt buried itself deeply inside her.

Immediately, the wife disclosed the dilemma to her husband, who attempted to share scriptures about how God would forgive them if they asked him, only to realize that he needed much more persuasion and wisdom than he possessed in order to resolve the matter. Plus, she and the husband knew if they sought spiritual guidance from their active membership, the advice would insist on immediate dissolution of their marriage. So the husband suggested meeting with a preacher from another affiliation who had no reason to be biased or sensitive towards their circumstance—one who owed them nothing (nothing but the truth, that is), and that the church affiliation shared the same plan of salvation as their current institution did.

The couple met with a local preacher, who not only fitted their criteria, but also expressed his views quite candidly concerning marriage, divorce, and remarriage. He used *Matthew 19* to show the advocating circumstance that allowed divorce, and when violated, the sin it manifested. Next, the preacher said that they should not have divorced their previous spouses without knowing in their heart that they had been betrayed (although unfaithfulness is very active in today's marriages, most accusers can only rely on circumstantial evidence apart from confessional or visional support), and that they should've stayed single or reconciled with their mates. Those options were gone since both "ex's" were married to other people and they themselves were married, too.

Still convicted, the wife asked, "How could they remain together if God considers their marriage to be no good?" The preacher's reply stated that God recognizes and judges a divorce to be a divorce, and a marriage to be a marriage, regardless of the reasons why. If this was not so, then God could not convict anyone on divorce or adultery if he does not recognize every kind of divorce, and every kind of marriage between a man and woman. Jesus sheds light on this matter. (*Matt. 19:6 ". . . what therefore God hath joined together, let no man put asunder"*) Jesus reveals that man has the choice and ability to separate what God joined together. And while God does recognize a divorce and marriage to be valid, this does not mean we have his support when the divorce or marriage is spiritual illegal.

More on this matter: (*1 Corinthians 7:14 "For the unbelieving husband is sanctified by the wife, and the unbelieving wife is sanctified by the husband; else were your children unclean; but now are they holy"*) That last phrase, *"but now are they holy,"* is the same reason the distraught couple's marriage can be acceptable and holy unto God.

In '*1 Corinthians*' it was through the righteousness of the spouse that made the marriage honorable, even though the one spouse defiled it. Under the same circumstance, the distraught couple's marriage is made honorable through their union in Christ, even though they defiled it.

The only question left is what they should do now, and what steps they should take to prevent from falling into the hands of an eternal God, who assures he has a place of everlasting punishment for adulterers. Let's agree that no sin today is completely dealt with until confession and repentance is rendered. The God we serve has provided the wonderful sacrifice of atonement for our sins. And although he loves us dearly, we still have to acknowledge when we're wrong as part of making it right. (*Jeremiah 3:12 ". . . Return, thou backsliding Israel, saith the Lord; and I will not cause mine anger to fall upon you: for I am merciful, saith the Lord, and I will not keep anger forever" 3:13 "only acknowledge thine iniquity, that thou hast transgressed against the Lord thy God . . ."*)

Once we take the proper measures to satisfy our God, we'll be able to experience peace again and move forward. (*Psalms 32:1 "Blessed is he whose transgression is forgiven, whose sin is covered" 32:5 "I acknowledged my sin unto thee, and mine iniquity I have not hid. I said, I will confess my transgressions unto the Lord; and thou forgavest the iniquity of my sin . . ."*) And there are more passages that urge us to go to God when we violate his commandments. (*1 John 1:9 "If we confess our sins, he is faithful and just to forgive us our sins, and to cleanse us from all unrighteousness" Isaiah 1:18 "Come now, and let us reason together, saith the Lord: though your sins be as scarlet, they shall be white as snow . . ." Galatians 2:21 "I do not frustrate the grace of God: for if righteous come by law, then Christ is dead in vain"*)

At the end of the meeting between the preacher and married couple, the wife still wasn't comfortable with the preacher's final and blunt suggestion of, "Get on with your marriage." Days and weeks went by with the same convictions occasionally surfacing in the marriage and often disrupting their relationship for extensive periods. Not sure what the impact or outcome would be, the husband openly emailed their dilemma to two more ministers of international influence. While waiting for the ministers' response, the husband searched and shared every scriptural passage he could find that would advocate the maintaining of their marriage. Finally, after checking his emails profusely, the international ministers replied. The first email was short and to the point—"Two wrongs don't make a right. Accept God's grace and move on." Plus, that minister mailed study pamphlets on the subject of God's grace. The second email elaborated on similar passages that focused on God's grace as well, and his willingness to forgive them of their past sins. That evangelist suggested counseling from their pastor in the matter as well.

While the communication and feedback from the preacher and ministers played a huge part in clearing up most of the doubt and guilt for the wife, *Matthew 19:2* revealed a much-needed piece of information that should've been discovered by the couple a long time ago. (*Matt. 19:2 "And great multitudes followed him . . ."*) In this chapter the location had nothing to do with the

Pharisees wanting to challenge Jesus, it was the number of witnesses they could use to discredit his teachings. (*Matt. 19:3 "The Pharisees also came unto him, tempting him, and saying unto him, 'Is it lawful for a man to divorce his wife for every cause?'"*)

Isn't it ironic that after Jesus explains the *Do's* and *Don'ts* of marriage and divorce—who commits adultery, and how it's committed? How the two fleshes become one, and that no man should divide what God has joined together? Isn't it weird that there's no recording of any couples separating as a result of Jesus' teachings on the subject?

All through the 'New Testament' we find recordings of what one person did or didn't do as a result of his belief. We find recordings of what groups did or didn't do as a result of their belief, and we even find recordings of what nations did or didn't do as a result of their belief. Yet, we find no recordings of any unlawfully married couples leaving their spouses after Jesus addresses the Pharisees and the multitude. Neither are there any recordings of examples in the 'New Testament' where any unlawfully married couples broke their vows and lived single lives in order to make things right with God. Surely one would think if this was such a common and serious practice that's going to thrust millions of Christians into hell, *Luke, Peter, Paul, James* and *John* would've at least mention it in one of their epistles?

Some married couples who are struggling with this problem tend to believe they can divorce their current spouses and ask God to forgive them for it, and then the matter is resolved. It's unfortunate that the couples are more concerned about the *unlawful marriages* than they are with the *unlawful divorces*. But what they fail to realize is if they qualify to receive forgiveness for one part of the violation, they have to qualify to receive forgiveness for the other part also in order to be whole again.

God can't forgive people for unlawful divorces without forgiving them for unlawful marriages—the two go hand-in-hand. You either receive forgiveness for both violations when confession is made, or you don't for either.

++ To recommend that a current married couple nullify their marriage because they didn't divorce correctly in a previous marriage, violating the terms of permission, is a step backward and supports *'St. Mark'* to the fullest. (*Mark 7:7 ". . . teaching for doctrines the commandments of men" Mark 7:9 ". . . that you may keep your own tradition").* Jesus' blood was so pure, perfect and powerful that it cleanses believers of all sins—past, present and future. The only two sins the blood of Christ does not atone for is *'Unbelief' (John 3:18 ". . . but he that believeth not is condemned already, because he hath not believed in the name of the only begotten Son of God"),* and *'Blasphemy'* of the Holy Spirit. (*Mark 3:29 "But he that shall blaspheme against the Holy Ghost hath never forgiveness . . .")* And these are the two categories Jesus himself judged to be unforgivable, not the sins man attempts to add to the list.

Anyway, the earlier distraught couple still remains peacefully married.

Is the Name of a Church Assembly essential to Salvation, and Must a Person be Baptized Again if the Affiliation Refuses to Honor It

Although no church establishment openly advertises their belief on these topics, I have encountered one affiliation that proclaims to be literally, by name, the Lord's Church. It discredits all other banners millions of Christians walk under each weekend and even declines invitations to worship in unaffiliated assemblies. In addition to that summery, a few of its members still recommend a person to acquire a second baptism from their institution if the previous baptism was administered outside of their affiliation.

Is there great division within the church colonies? Yes. But if one affiliation exalts itself above all others, it will automatically attach the congregation to a lifetime of defense. Before we arrive at any conclusions, we must treat these topics as we did the others and examine where the teachings originated, and why some Christians continue to hold firmly to this belief.

Yes, human beings are taught that every person is created equal. But what might set them apart from each other may or may not depend on race, nationality, gender, achievements, and of course, religion. Still, we refuse to accept any proclamations without proof. If someone says they're the greatest basketball player in the world, they had better provide the stats to go with it. If another person brags on her intellect, she better have some kind of way to prove her level of I.Q. If someone is accused of a crime, the prosecutor must obtain sufficient evidence if he's going to win the case.

Anytime a person or group of people proclaim to be superior over another person or group of people, they will have opened themselves up to an enormous amount of scrutiny. Criticism will arise from every arena in order to make them either denounce their claim, or prove what they say is true. That's exactly what frustrated the Pharisees and Jews about Jesus' proclamation. (*John 5:18 ". . . but said also that God was his Father, making himself equal with God" 10:33 ". . . 'For good work we stone you not; but for blasphemy; and because that thou, being a man, makest thyself God.'* ") This claim was so farfetched that it was even illegal to utter the words. (*Luke 5:21 "And the scribes and the Pharisees began to reason, saying, 'Who is this which speaketh blasphemy' . . ."*)

Jesus also addressed the issue when people thought they were better than others. (*Luke, 18:9 "And he spake this parable unto certain which trusted in themselves that they were righteous, and despised others" 18:14 ". . . for everyone that exalteth himself shall be abased; and he that humbleth himself shall be exalted."*) It's plainly spoken in the Bible about Christians who promote these kinds of teachings. (*Mark 7:6 ". . . this people honoureth me with their lips, but their heart is far from me" Isaiah 65:5 ". . . for I am holier than thou. These are a smoke in my nose, a fire that burneth all day."*)

After attentively listening to one church's sermon and sitting in on months of Bible study, I occasionally heard faithful members acknowledge and campaign their assembly to be the 'Lord's Church' by name primarily because of one scriptural passage. (*Matt. 16:18 "And I say unto thee, 'That thou art Peter, and upon this rock I will build my church; and the gates of hell shall not prevail against it.'* ")

Is this the defining moment when Jesus decrees all synagogues and churches, which don't display his name in bold italics, to be denounced as an acceptable place-of-worship? If he did, then Jesus chose an individual, who just hours away, would deny having had anything to do with him. (*Matt. 26:75 "And Peter remembered the word of Jesus, which said unto him, 'Before the cock crow, thou shalt deny me thrice.' And he went out, and he wept bitterly.'* ") We all know how the story ends with Christ resurrecting, appearing to the remaining eleven apostles, and quizzing this same *Peter* three times about his love for him. (*John 21:17 "He saith unto him the third time, 'Simon, son of Jonas, lovest thou me?' Peter was grieved because he said unto him the third time, 'Lovest thou me?' And he said unto him, 'Lord, thou knowest all things; thou knowest that I love thee.' Jesus saith unto him, 'Feed my sheep.' "*)

If Jesus had not resurrected, then *Peter* might've been able to justify or at least hide his secret of denying him. But under these circumstances, *Peter* had no choice but to openly deal with it the way he and Christ were doing. Jesus knew he was the Head of the Church, and if *Peter* was going to be the person identified representing the principles it was going to be built upon, then *Peter* could no longer act as a coward or traitor toward truth. And the only way believers were going to withstand the coming persecutions was for *Peter* and the other apostles to equip them with the gospel: *"Feed my sheep."* Which gives believers the strength, courage, and faith needed in order to keep the 'gates-of-hell' from prevailing against them.

Isn't it a little surprising that *Peter* writes two epistles to the Christians of his time, with the heart of both letters placing emphasis on the need for believers to be courageous and remain faithful under persecution, along with his attack on false teachers? Why didn't *Peter* use his fifteen hundred years of fame to boast or remind his readers that Jesus chose him to build his church on?

While it's factual that Jesus does identify his church to be built upon *Peter's* shoulders, it does not insinuate that every church building must stamp J.C. on their stationery in order to be recognized as an official place-of-worship. What made Jesus confirm *Peter's* reply to be accurate of who he was, is because *Peter* acknowledged him to be God's son. (*Matt. 16:16 "And Simon Peter answered and said, 'Thou art the Christ, the Son of the living God.' "*) Even with *Peter's* correct assumption of who Jesus was, *Peter* does not receive credit for originally knowing the answer. (*Matt. 16:17 ". . . blessed art thou, Simon Barjona: for flesh and blood hath not revealed it unto thee, but my Father which is in heaven."*)

So now we know it's safe to say if there was a church institution out there that could rightfully claim to be the one affiliation who Jesus endorses as his church, then it would be revealed by the Father or by Jesus himself, not through the interpretation of a prejudiced organization. Also when

Jesus tells *Peter*, "Upon this rock I shall build my church," he's talking about using the bold, confident, humble, and loving personality *Peter* will later possess as examples of the characteristics his church shall be developed upon; not by the religious title of an affiliation.

But some members of 'non-denominational' affiliations will stand behind the claim that their church institution's name is based on a biblical identity (*Romans 16:16 ". . . the churches of Christ salute you"*); whereas most of today's churches are not, and don't qualify to advertise themselves as a 'right' place-of-worship. If this is true, then I'm afraid many nationalities won't make the heavenly roster since they're not mentioned either in the Bible. Americans, Japanese, Jamaicans, Australians, and all the other hundreds of nations around the world are not mentioned as well.

The *church of Christ* is not the only church assembly mentioned in the New Testament. There are several more church institutions identified by their states and towns instead of *church of Christ (Romans 16:4 ". . . unto whom not only I give thanks, but also all the churches of the Gentiles" 1 Corinthians 1:2 "unto the church of God" Galatians 1:2 ". . . unto the churches of Galatia" 1 Thessalonians 1:1 ". . . unto the church of the Thessalonians . . ."*), and that's not including those in the book of *Revelations*. There's even passages that suggest the 'church' to be in someone's home, referring to people. (*Philemon 1:2 "And to our beloved Apphia . . ., and to the church in thy house" Romans 16:5 "Likewise greet the church that is in their house . . ."*) If we're attempting to give *'special privileges'* to one group, affiliation, or person based solely on a biblical identity, then we cannot honor the process of elimination in one scenario and overrule it in another. Either the biblical identities matter (based solely on names) or they don't.

Thousands of years ago God chose and made one nation of people elite to the rest of the world, but that was because he was initially establishing his identity and power to the world through a particular group of people. After Jesus' birth, death and resurrection, nations, groups, and every person lost the right to claim being God's only masterpiece, because God is not prejudice or discriminative. His grace included every one: *John 3:16 "For God so loved the world . . ."*

The Jews attempted to hold on to their one-time privilege by decreeing physical circumcision on the Gentiles as a requirement for God to accept them. But *Paul* explains how circumcision holds its valued identity, and how its valued identity is also lost: (*Romans 2:25 "For circumcision verily profiteth, if thou keep the law: but if thou be a breaker of the law, thy circumcision is made uncircumcision"*). *Paul* is stating that although you are a part of a group based on your legal identity, there are spiritual stipulations that nullify your accepted mark of circumcision, which abolishes you from the establishment. Yet, in another passage we read that if you are not originally or legally identified by a superficial criteria, but are one who obeys God's law, you will be adopted and accepted into His establishment; even though you're not identical to the rest of the group: (*Romans 2:26 "Therefore if the uncircumcision keep the righteousness of the law, shall not his uncircumcision be counted for circumcision?" Romans 2:29 "But he is a Jew, which is one inwardly; and circumcision is that of the heart, in the spirit, and not in the letter; whose praise is not of men, but of God"*). Outside identity is not where value registers with God. It is one's content, sincerity, obedience, and faith that appeases him.

Although names are extremely significant in the *natural* world, in the *supernatural* world, except for God, Jesus and the Holy Spirit, they hold very little prestige and are almost irrelevant. (*Luke 16:15 "... for that which is highly esteemed among men is abomination in the sight of God."*) When Moses evaluated God's will for him to return to Egypt and free the Israelites from Pharaoh, he questioned God's identity by needing a name. (*Exodus 3:13 "... what is his name? what shall I say unto them?" 3:14 "And God said unto Moses, 'I AM THAT I AM' ... 'I AM hath sent me unto you.'"*) God knowing the hearts of men added the more typical way to identify himself to the Israelites. (*Exodus 3:15 "... the Lord God of your fathers, the God of Abraham, the God of Isaac, and the God of Jacob, hath sent me unto you ..."*)

People on earth place enormous attention and responsibility on names, whereas in the spiritual world, it's not that big-a-deal. Look at *Jacob* when he wrestled the angel: he desired greatly to know the angel's name after it bruised his hip, but to no avail. (*Genesis 32:28 "And he said, 'Thy name shall be called no more Jacob, but Israel: for as a prince hast thou power with God and with man, and have prevailed'" 32:29 "And*

40

Jacob asked him, and said, 'Tell me, I pray thee, thy name'" And he said, 'Wherefore is it that thou dost ask after my name . . .?'") Throughout the book of *'Revelations'* with all its angels, elders, six-winged creatures, dragons, the *Lamb*, riders on different colored horses, and *He* who sits on the throne, *John* hardly identifies anyone by name.

Even though the 'New Jerusalem' came down from heaven, and on its twelve gates were written names of the twelve tribes of Israel, and its wall was built on stones with the names of the twelve apostles; apart from that, there isn't much attention given to actual names. However, obedience, purpose, and effect does seem to be the nucleus that's going to outweigh 'names' at the end of time.

The struggle of deciding where 'place-of-worship' is accepted by God has been around for centuries. Even Jesus and the Samarian woman at the well were eventually divided over the above claim. After Jesus revealed to the woman her circumstances surrounding her five husbands and one roommate, she realized that Jesus had the ability to look into the past, prove the present, and prophesy the future (*John 4:19 "The woman saith unto him, 'Sir I perceived that thou art a prophet"*).

Isn't it odd that the woman could've asked Jesus a hundred questions about the mysteries of her past, events of that day, and also find out what's going to happen to her investment next month? But, instead, she chose to sought the truth concerning where the right 'place-of-worship' was located. (*John 4:20 "Our fathers worshipped in this mountain; and ye say, that in Jerusalem is the place where men ought to worship."*) Jesus' stern reply advises her to forget all scholars she's heard and focus on his information only. (*John 4:21 "Jesus saith unto her, 'Woman, believe me, the hour cometh, when ye shall neither in this mountain, nor yet at Jerusalem, worship the Father.' "*)

Jesus even had to confront his disciples about their excessive pride in their 'place-of-worship.' (*Matthew 24:1-2 ". . . and his disciples came to him for to shew him the building of the temple—and Jesus said unto them, 'See ye not all these things verily I say unto you, there shall not be left here one stone upon another, that shall not be thrown down.' "*) Jesus released everyone from external inspirations and directed them toward a more essential and effective way of worshipping God. (*John*

4:23-24 *"But the hour cometh, and now is, when the true worshippers shall worship the Father in spirit and in truth: for the Father seeketh such to worship him—God is Spirit: and they that worship him must worship him in spirit and in truth."*)

++ For anyone to boast or believe their 'place-of-worship' is the holy-of-holies, has obviously missed the focal point in several of Jesus' teachings. For instance, 'The Good Samarian.' (*Luke 10:30 "And Jesus answering said, 'A certain man went down from Jerusalem to Jericho, and fell among thieves . . . leaving him half dead.' "*) We know from the whole story that three people (a Levite, a priest, and a Samarian) came across a man in need. The person who the Jews despised over the two men they respected, was the individual praised for conducting the neighborly act. Again, we read where Jesus explains that his Father does not judge by external attributes. One man informed Jesus that his mother and brother were waiting outside and wanted to speak with him. (*Matt. 12:48 "But he answered and said unto him that told him, 'Who is my mother? And who is my brethren?'"* 12:50 *"For whosoever shall do the will of my Father which is in heaven, the same is my brother, and sister, and mother."*)

What *'Deuteronomy 10:17'* and the above scriptures have in common is that they show God is not a respecter of person, title, relationship or place when it comes to glorifying him. All are equal.

There are many Christians who will go to their grave teaching and believing that salvation includes the right place of worship based on biblical identity. I personally corresponded with an author through emails concerning a Christian magazine article he wrote: *"The Name of the Church is a Big Deal."* I won't mention the Magazine by name or the Author. Written below will be most of our conversation after I identified myself.

me: I'm starting by asking you does the Name on the Building where people worship dictate or determine their qualification for eternity in Heaven? Are many Christians making too much noise about this issue for no reason that matters to God, or are many devoted Christians going to be forever lost simply based on the banner they walk underneath each weekend? I also explained some of the scenarios that you've read from my book on this topic and shared to him how these illustrations were in the Bible to help Christians stay unified, not divided. I concluded that "the name of the church anyone worships inside will not be a factor as long as they are teaching, absorbing, and living the Gospel of Jesus Christ."

MA: I do not shy away from being distinctive in the places the gospel is distinctive. I too am concerned that too many think walking under a 'Church of Christ' sign will save them. What is taught inside matters, obeying the true gospel and living with the aim of Christ-likeness must be the pursuit of us all. My article was simply showing that we must be scriptural as we refer to the church the Lord died to save. Could we call the church 'Joe Blow' as long as truth is taught inside? I was simply stressing in the article that Christ has one church, it belongs to Him; and any scriptural designation we give should glorify Him.

me: I guess I am still asking does the name of the building where Christians worship inside have merit towards their qualifications to obtain eternity or not? Many people are advertising that if you do not belong to the 'Church of Christ' (place-of-worship), you will not go to heaven. Do you agree, or are they intentionally leaving out what this saying really means and promoting their institution through the ignorance of others? I am not saying that people are thinking that worshipping inside a Church of Christ building is what saves them. I know Christians are a sanctified people, and not everyone who says, *"Lord, Lord, will enter into the Kingdom . . ."* But that passage is not based on which church facility we worship God inside. All Christians are the Body of Christ *(Ephes. 1:23)*. The Magazine Author then left the primary question about the name of the worship center and asked me my plan of salvation. "Does it include baptism or not?" Well, as you all know from reading my book, I do promote baptism as a part of obedience to God's word. I do not know the circumstances of an individual if he is imprisoned and dies before he is baptized. Likewise, if a woman lies in a hospital bed and obeys the gospel, but yet, passes away in her sleep before baptism. I cannot judge if grace will sustain her or not; it is really none of my business. Jesus reprimanded his disciples about being overly concerned or judgmental about the eternal fate of another person; in this case—Judas: *(John 21:21 "Peter seeing him saith to Jesus, Lord, and what shall this man do?" 21:22 "Jesus saith unto him, If I will that he tarry til I come, what* *is that to thee . . .?").* I had to clarify some of this in my response email. And then I wrote: *"What does my belief on baptism have to do with my question about the name of the building being essential to salvation?"*

MA: To me, this is the fundamental difference in what I believe and what denominations teach and practice. I do not believe the 'Sinner's Prayer'. And to answer your question, "No," I do not believe the name of the building has merit by itself toward a person's qualifications to obtain eternity. What I mean is we must be scriptural in all we do, including how we refer to the church belonging to Christ. But a person should not think he is going to be saved simply because he attends a church with the "right name." We need to be clear with people when we speak of the Church of Christ. I do not believe the Church of Christ includes those who believe and practice the errors of denominationalism. If a person after becoming a Christian deliberately designates or consents to a local church call the "Joe Blow" or "Lutheran Church" (neither Joe or Lutheran died to purchase it), I do believe his soul would be in jeopardy. I am a sincere man who loves the Lord. I do not follow a movement. I am converted to Christ. I am not converted to a group of churches called "Church of Christ." I disagree with a number of churches with that name. I follow the King. I have joined myself to a local Church of Christ and I believe they are His.

++ me: You said, *"No, you don't believe the name of the building has merit by itself toward a person's qualifications to obtain eternity."* Do you not see the problem in your statement? No concrete, wood or metal building has MERIT at all, let alone by itself when it comes to a person's salvation. I hope this simplifies my question and your answer. It's not, I repeat, it's not the name of the church building that matters, but who is the HEAD (Jesus). The Bible places its emphasis on Christ being the Head of His Church over the name of the assembly. Christ is more interested in returning to gather his Church where he is the Head of the Body rather than where his name is dried in paint. However, if you believe and are comfortable where you worship our Lord and Savior Jesus Christ, then keep doing it there. But you cannot sit on God's throne and judge your Christian brothers and sisters who do worship the same God of Abraham, Isaac and Jacob as you do under the roof of another building that waits to be destroyed at the end of time, just like yours. Read Romans 14 and understand how one man's faith does not convict another man's different faith. Just when I thought the conversations were getting good, I never heard from the magazine author again. Please, everyone, remember *Romans 2:25-26* as part of your identity to Christ.

++ God knows how puffed up we become once we think we're in a class by ourselves. Elijah thought he was solitary in God's service until God told him that he wasn't: (*1 Kings 19:10 ". . . and I, even I alone am left . . ." 19:18 "Yet I have left me seven thousand in Israel, all the knees which have not bowed unto Baal . . ."*). Even if there were a church affiliation out there that God favored, it still would lack something to keep it from boasting supremacy. (*Revelation 3:1 "And unto the angel of the church in Sardis write . . ." 3:2 ". . . for I have not found thy works perfect before God"*)

The notion of someone being required to be a member of a particular church affiliation in order to complete their qualification as a candidate for heaven, is no more misleading than the Jews suggesting the Gentiles to be circumcised during their era. Also, these man-made rules insult Jesus by portraying his death, burial and resurrection to be not good enough for the Father, while taunting the Christian's faith in him as well. And finally, what did Jesus mean when he told his disciples, *"And if I go and prepare a place for you, I will come again, and receive you unto myself; that where I am, there ye may be also" John 14:3.* Jesus died for people, and for people only. He is returning to gather people, not bricks, pews, pulpits and stained-glass windows. Be wise; nothing Jesus died for had anything to do with the church building we worship inside.

Unfortunately, a **dishonored baptism** usually stems from our earlier discussion. Normally, when a second baptism is administered it is because the person acknowledges that they did not initially understand the true aspects of its purpose. It is this understanding and conviction, led by the desire to voluntarily do things correctly, that demands a second baptism. It's not by the judgment or condemnation of a church affiliation who rules it to be unacceptable to God because they didn't perform it.

Even though we've already covered the topic of baptism in an earlier chapter, trickling complications continue to stunt our growth and delay many Christians from arriving at a spiritual maturity. If a person visits one thousand different church facilities he would discover about two-thirds of the structures do house a glass pool behind the pulpit, utilized for the purpose of baptizing. The remaining church facilities that do not possess a glass pool have other ways to access water for baptism.

All church problems do not exist because certain institutions teach baptism, and others don't. Another problem arises when a person has been baptized by an outside affiliation, and the new affiliation has to decide if they'll accept it as sufficient for that person in obeying the Gospel.

Isn't it appalling how some affiliations will denounce a baptism performed in the name of the Father, the Son, and the Holy Ghost by an outside, ordained minister, yet embrace a couple married by an atheist justice-of-the-peace or notary public? Why not rule that insufficient? Do some church congregations really possess that much animosity against another congregation? Let's attempt to close the gap on this conflicting belief so all Christians can know where they stand with God on honorable baptisms.

We know God directed *Paul* to some of the Gentile nations, which inspired him to write letters to different churches or visit them. But the *Galatians'* debate over the belief that a person had to do more than have faith in Christ in order to be put right with God, compelled *Paul* to judged the meritless claim as being concocted by false teachers. Fortunately, we're able to extract from *Paul's* explanation how a person is put right with God, the understanding of what baptism qualifies us for, and its approval into a relationship with our Creator. (*Galatians 3:27 "For as many of you as have been baptized into Christ have put on Christ" 3:28 "There is neither Jew nor Greek, there is neither bond nor free, there is neither male nor female: for ye all are one in Christ."*)

Jesus had to correct his disciples again when they felt their deputation was being shared and interfered with by outsiders. (*Mark 9:38 "And John, answered him, saying, 'Master, we saw one casting out devils in thy name, and he followeth not us: and we forbad him, because he followeth not us.'"*) Jesus shows the disciples they have the wrong attitude about the work of the Kingdom and instructs them not to forbid the person just because he doesn't belong to their clique. (*Mark 9:40 "For he that is not against us is our part."*)

Paul's first letter to the 'Corinthians' involved dealing with division within the church because some Christians believed the standard was set by whoever a person was baptized by. (*1 Corinthians 1:10 "Now I beseech you, brethren, by the name of Christ, that you all speak the same thing, and that there be no divisions among you . . ." 1:13 "Is Christ divided—was Paul crucified for you? or were you baptized in the name of Paul" 1:14 "I thank God that I baptized none of you, but Crispus and Gaius."*)

++ The understanding I receive, through the examination of the passages, suggest that all affiliations which teach and preach the gospel of Jesus Christ are well-accepted as a right place of worship: including their baptism. And all people who believe and obey the gospel are accepted into citizenship of the 'Just'.

Is it the Holy Spirit that We Hear, or Just Our Conscience

Although the pacing of this topic changes dramatically from the last one, it does not draw affiliations any closer to a peace treaty. And when someone attempts to explain the *Yes* and *No's* of this conflict in belief, they had better be ready for their views to be critiqued thoroughly by mankind, and by God. This is no ordinary or easy topic to breakdown, especially when speaking evil of the Holy Spirit implements the *unpardonable sin*. So I'm going to focus on limiting my elaborations and allow scriptures to dominate the input, while letting God's Spirit lead in what you need to know apart from my interpretations.

How many times have we said or at least heard someone say, "The Spirit told me, or something told me, or I heard a voice?" Ironically, the confusion is not usually tied to the person who makes the claim, but to the listener. I'm not sure that when a person opens his conversation with this claim it's because he's reassuring the listener of what he's about to profess, or if he's emphasizing the value of it. It may even be a representation of the relationship he has with God. But whatever inspires a person to use the Holy Spirit as their reason for hearing what they heard, it certainly makes the listeners judge their information to be highly dependable, or just plain self-promoted.

But how could one Christian believe God's Spirit communicates intimately and internally with people while another Christian doesn't? The dividing factor could have a lot more to do experience itself rather than doctrinal teachings. Even though ancient Israel once accepted and revered the prophets God spoke through, we read in the 'Old Testament' that Israel also had similar problems with its prophets claiming to have heard from God, when actually they didn't: (*Jeremiah 23:16 "Thus saith the Lord of hosts, Hearken not unto the words of the prophets that prophesy unto you: they make you vain: they speak a vision of their own heart, and not out of the mouth of the Lord" 23:21 ". . . I have not spoken to them, yet they prophesy"*).

This behavior made false prophesies linger a long time, especially when some predictions were geared toward the latter future—sort of compared with a woman professing to be pregnant, and for a short time, the father-to-be would have to just take her word. However, God used a specific method to validate when people claimed he spoke to them: (*Jeremiah 28:9 ". . . when the word of the prophet shall come to pass, then shall the prophet be known, that the Lord hath truly sent him" Deuteronomy 18:22 "When a prophet speaketh in the name of the Lord, if the thing follow not, nor come to pass, that is the thing which the Lord hath not spoken, but the prophet hath spoken it presumptuously . . ."*).

The Bible also has scriptures that display evidence of God personally communicating with man through dreams, (*Jeremiah 23:28 "The prophet that hath a dream, let him tell a dream; and he that hath my word, let him speak my word faithfully . . ."*) by visions, (*Isaiah 1:1 "The vision of Isaiah the son of Amoz" Acts 2:17 "And it shall come to pass in the last days, saith God, I will pour out my Spirit upon all flesh . . . and your young men shall see visions . . ."*), and even face to face as the case was with Moses: (*Exodus 33:11 "And the Lord spake unto Moses face to face, as a man speaketh unto his friend . . ."*).

Jesus assured his disciples that after his death he would send the *Holy Spirit* to believers on earth. (*John 16:7 ". . . it is expedient for you that I go away: for if I go not away, the Comforter will not come unto you; but if I depart, I will send him unto you" 14:16 "And I will pray the Father, and he shall give you another Comforter, that he may abide with you forever" 14:17 "Even the Spirit of truth; whom the world cannot receive, because it seeth him not, neither knoweth him: but ye know him; for he dwelleth with you and shall be in you" 14:26 "But the Comforter, which is the Holy Ghost, whom the Father will send in my name . . ." Luke 24:49 "And behold I send the promise of my Father upon you: but tarry in the city of Jerusalem . . ."*)

Indeed we read that the *Holy Spirit* was bestowed on the disciples by Jesus (*John 20:22 "And when he had said this, he breathed on them, and said unto them, 'Receive ye the Holy Ghost.' "*), as well as 3000 believers on the Day-of-Pentecost. (*Acts 2:38 "Then Peter said unto them, 'Repent, and be baptized everyone of you in the name of Jesus Christ for the remission of sins, and ye shall receive the gift of the Holy Ghost'" 2:41 ". . . and that same day there were added unto them about three thousand souls."*)

There are several verses in the 'New Testament' that proclaim the dwelling of the Spirit to be housed inside Christians as some understand it (*1 Corinthians 3:16 "Know ye not that ye are the temple of God, and that the Spirit of God dwelleth in you" Isaiah 57:15 ". . . I dwell in the high and holy place, with him also that is of a contrite and humble spirit . . ." John 14:17 ". . . but ye know him; for he dwelleth with you, and shall be in you"*), and there are other passages that link the Spirit to dwelling inside Christians. (*Ephesians 3:16 ". . . to be strengthened with might by his Spirit in the inner man" 3:17 "That Christ may dwell in your hearts by faith . . ."*) If someone advises Christians to not take "the dwelling of the Spirit" literally as living inside them, then in the same breath they must also advise them to not take "the dwelling of sin" literally as living inside them either. (*Romans 7:17 "Now then it is no more I that do it, but sin that dwelleth in me" 7:20 "Now if I do that I would not, it is no more I that do it, but sin that dwelleth in me."*) You cannot split the word "dwelleth" into two scenarios or definitions when the sentences are referring to the same behavior, especially when the behavior includes 'abiding' inside a specific territory.

Even when it pertains to demonic spirits, they've possessed the ability to speak on earth, and sometimes to mankind as well as through mankind. (*1 Chronicles 21:1 "And Satan stood up against Israel, and provoked David to number Israel" John 13:26 ". . . and when he had dipped the sop, he gave it to Judas Iscariot—13:27 "And after the sop Satan entered into him . . ." Matt. 16:22 "Then Peter took him, and began to rebuke him, saying, 'Be it far from thee, Lord: this shall not be unto you'" 16:23 "But he turned, and said unto Peter, 'Get thee behind me, Satan: thou art an offence unto me' . . ."*) The Bible also shares one story about many demons housing themselves inside a mad man until Jesus rebukes them. (*Mark 5:9 "And he asked him, 'What is thy name? and he answered saying,' "My name is Legion: for we are many" Matt. 12:43 "When an unclean spirit is gone out of a man . . ." 12:44 "Then he saith, 'I will return into my house from whence I came out' . . .")* So we do have evidence that a spirit can penetrate the human body.

Last but not least, we have a passage that implicates 'King Saul' using a medium to contact a deceased prophet to advise him during a crisis. (*1 Samuel 28:3 "Now Samuel was dead and all Israel had lamented him, and buried him in Ramah . . ." 28:7 "Then said Saul unto his servants, 'Seek me a woman that hath a familiar spirit, that I may go to her'" 28:8 ". . . he said, 'I pray thee, divine unto me by the familiar spirit, and bring me him up, whom I shall name unto thee'"*) As the story goes the medium summons the prophet from the afterlife and he speaks to 'King Saul'. (*1 Samuel 28:15 "And Samuel said to Saul, 'Why hast thou disquieted me, to bring me up . . .?' "*)

What I'm asking is why would God enable unclean spirits to communicate with mankind, and yet prohibit his own Spirit from accessing them, which were created in His image? Or if God did allow his Spirit to communicate directly with man at one time, what made him change the routine? Do we not have more access to every heavenly blessing, now that Christ has risen from death and sits on the right side of the Father? (*Ephesians 1:3 "Blessed be the God and Father of our Lord Jesus Christ, who hath blessed us with all spiritual blessings in heavenly places with Christ."*) Are those spiritual blessings limited to hearing directly from God's Holy Spirit?

Some preachers discredit any direct communications by the Holy Spirit to believers because of one single passage. (*1 Corinthians 13:10 "But that which is perfect is come, then that which is in part shall be done away."*) But "that which is perfect is come" hasn't always come with a unified interpretation. Some Christians profess "that which is perfect is come" to be Christ on his first visit among human beings, while other Christians believe "that which is perfect is come" to be the completion of the Bible—mainly the New Testament. In either case this passage is sufficient enough for some affiliations to teach that many of the *Holy Spirit's* attributes have ceased as of centuries ago, including hearing from Him.

"That which is perfect is come" could not have been Christ because *Paul* didn't say, "He which is perfect." Yes, when Christ visited man, he was perfect in terms of performing miracles no one had performed before, and did not commit any sins, which led to his being the perfect sacrifice who always pleased the Father. But Christ did not become absolutely perfect again in terms of heavenly standards until after his death, not during his 3 ½ year missionary. Every human being lacks a particular perfection as long as they remain on earth. (*Luke 7:28 ". . . among those that are born of women there is not a greater prophet than John the Baptist: but he that is least in the kingdom of God is greater than he."*)

When *Mary Magdalene* attempted to touch Jesus upon his resurrection, he forbade her. Why? Because he was not yet perfect again: (*John 20:17 "Jesus said unto her, 'Touch me not; for I am not yet ascended to my Father' . . ."*). Remember just three days ago Jesus had taken on the sins of the world, and during his missionary experienced earthly things that may have kept him from being supernaturally pure and perfected in the way he was before he arrived: (*John 17:5 ". . . 'O Father, glorify thou me with thine own self with the glory which I had with thee before the world was"*). This temporarily contamination could've manifested through the woman with the issue of blood: (*Luke 8:43 "And a woman had an issue of blood twelve years . . ." 8:44 "Came behind him, and touched the border of his garment . . ."*). Or it could be something as unacceptable as Judas' kiss of betrayal: (*Luke 22:48 "But Jesus said unto him, Judas, thou betrayest the Son of man with a kiss? "*). Plus, all through the Bible where we read prophesies pertaining to Jesus' manifestation on earth; none of the passages describe him as being the 'perfect' one.

When Jesus asked his disciples to tell him who people identified him as, they answered, (*Matt. 16:14 ". . . some say that thou art John the Baptist: some, Elias; and others Jeremias, or one of the prophets"*). Even when Jesus describes his own self, he does not attach his identity to the definition of 'perfect'. (*John 10:11 "I am the good shepherd . . ." 14:6 "I am the way, the truth, and the life . . ."*) Jesus and the people had plenty of opportunities to describe him as "that which is perfect is come," but all declined to do so. Jesus even goes as far as to reprimand one prominent gentleman for attempting to place him in that kind of category. (*Luke 18:18 "And a certain ruler asked him saying Good Master . . ." 18:19 "And Jesus said unto him, 'Why callest thou me good? None is good, save one, that is, God.'* ") He also enlightens us about the venerability of an earthly body. (*Matt. 26:41 ". . . the spirit is willing, but the flesh is weak."*) Still, this is the body type Christ was required to visit us wearing. (*John 1:1 "In the beginning was the Word, and the Word was with God, and the Word was God" 1:14 "And the Word was made flesh, and dwelt among us . . ."*) Obviously, this was a flesh that could be killed as well harmed. So "that which is perfect is come" could not have pertained to Christ's visit 2000 years ago.

As far as Christians choosing the completion of the Bible to represent "that which is perfect is come," the reality is that most theologians and scholars know the Bible was authored in the Hebrew, Greek and Aramaic language by many men, and these men were not the ones *Peter* was referring to in his epistle. (*2 Peter 1:21 "For the prophecy came not in the old time by the will of man: but holy men of God spake as they were moved by the Holy Ghost."*) That is partially the reason why some Bible translations do feature 'apocrypha' and 'deuterocanonical' books, and others do not.

++ And if there were any truth to man's interpretation of *Paul's* prophecy (*1 Cor. 13:10*) that meant certain gifts of the Holy Spirit would cease after the 'New Testament' was written and copied, then (*John 15:26-27 ". . . even the Spirit of truth, which proceedeth from the Father, he shall testify of me" . . . "And ye also shall bear witness . . ." John 17:20 "Neither pray I for these alone, but for them also which shall believe on me through their word"*) would have included the theory in their sentences. Because all of the above passages do refer to Jesus disclosing that the New Testament writings would come from his disciples. But Scripture does not indicate that the *Holy Spirit* would no longer speak to believers intimately once the last epistle was written or the last apostle has died. On the contrary, Scripture reveals just the opposite (*John 14:16 ". . . and he shall give you another Comforter, that he may abide with you forever" 14:17 ". . . for he shall dwelleth with you, and shall be in you"*). To teach that a Christian does not hear directly from the Holy Spirit, but discerns spiritual matters on his own, promotes too much self-praise and pride against God's wisdom. No person could come to the revelations and understandings of God's written word or the convictions and liberties he feels without the relationship of the *Holy Spirit*. Besides that, no earthly book could house all of God's wisdom, power, and plans.

The Bible does not explain or sum up everything about God. So this information, along with *Ephesians 1:9-10 & 1Cor. 13:12*, also helps rule out the Bible as being "that which is perfect is come." Plus, even with the Bible originating flawlessly, too many hands have now contaminated what many claim to be perfection. Also for an artifact to hold such dominant meaning and title, we could've expected the word 'Bible' to have appeared at least once in the Old or New Testament, right? "That which is perfect is come" is not an accurate account for whoever claims the prophecy in *1 Corinthians 13:10* foretold a black book would be its fulfillment. However, in these last days God does speak to us physically through the Bible, but he continues to speak to believes spiritually through his Spirit. The Bible is the primary method today to reveal the attitude, judgments, and righteousness of the Father. But the Spirit is the one who 'quickens' our understanding and consciousness of God's word. Millions of people read the Bible, but still cannot understand many of its teachings, why? The *Spirit* is the one who makes you see and hear what the flesh does not comprehend.

I have searched the Scriptures diligently for a quotation or passage that validates the claim that the *Holy Spirit* does not literally dwell inside the Christian, and that we hear only our own conscience. Since I did not find one, I must agree that all of the *Holy Spirit's* attributes are still obtainable to believers, especially hearing directly from him in the spirit.

One Day or Any Day for Communion

It would seem that when someone reads this title they will immediately perceive that I'm running out of things to discuss. However, the shameful fact is that church affiliations are divided 50-50 over the two thousand-year-old ritual, which is supposed to be the pinnacle reminder of the price Jesus paid in order for Christians to have a part in God's kingdom.

Communion has been controversial in its own way every since it was first introduced to the multitudes by Jesus himself. (*John 6:54 "Whoso eateth my flesh, and drinketh my blood, hath eternal life . . ."*) One reason Jesus' proclamation so widely misunderstood was because it was very hard to digest. (*John 6:60 "Many therefore of his disciples, when they heard this, said, 'This is an hard saying: who can hear it?' "*) Then Jesus attempts to relieve the people's confusion by explaining what he really meant. (*John 6:63 "It is the spirit that quickeneth; the flesh profiteth nothing: the words that I speak unto you, they are spirit, and they are life."*)

Communion is expressed with two symbols—bread, which represents Christ's body, and wine, which represents his blood: (*Matt. 26:26 "And as they were eating, Jesus took bread, and blessed it, and brake it, and gave it to the disciples, and said, 'Take, eat; this is my body' "*). Then he took a cup of wine and gave thanks, and said, (*Matt. 26:28 " For this is my blood of the new testament, which is shed for many the remission of sins"*). And finally we read the reason for this ritual to be implemented. (*1 Corinthians 11:24 ". . . this do in remembrance of me."*) Jesus chose two symbols to represent his sacrificial death, and has revealed to the world the purpose of Communion.

Although the *Lord's Supper* is very basic, many of its presentations are extremely formal. Some affiliations display Communion on immaculate tables and serve the unleavened bread and wine in vessels made of pure gold, while others may still draw the attention of Christians with ordinary dishes.

Over the centuries affiliations have added and subtracted ways to honor Communion. Unfortunately, some of these ways, such as the days and frequency it is offered, has provoked 'finger pointing' at churches because they either administer the *Lord's Supper* on days other than Sunday, or find no problem with Christians taking it as willfully as they desired.

What scriptural passage could cultivate a conclusion condemning Communion on any day other than Sunday? Perhaps these several verses have been a huge influence. (*1 Corinthians 10:16 ". . . the bread which we break, is it not the communion of the body of Christ?" Acts 20:7 "And upon the first day of the week, when the disciples came together to break bread . . ."*) There is no doubt that both passages are talking about the *Lord's Supper*. We are to certainly follow examples of the Apostles in whatever we are capable when it is specified as a commandment.

However, Jesus did use the term "*often* as you do it." We know it was not on the first day of the week when the ritual was first established in the upper room; neither was it done inside a church building. Plus, the disciples chose comfortably to administer Communion on a different day other than when it was originally presented to them as well.

Right now it's safe to say the disciples had to choose one of the seven days in a week to break bread because they couldn't create a new calendar day or add another one to the week. At some point they had to use one of the seven days as their day for Communion. If they had chosen Tuesday to take Communion, the argument would surround Communion on Tuesday as being the right day.

++ Just because the disciples picked Sunday as the days they administered the *Lord's Supper*, doesn't mean whoever doesn't follow this example to the 'T' will be condemned for breaking bread on another day. *Paul* elaborates on a similar situation involving days and months with the Galatians (*Galatians 4:9 ". . . how turn ye again to the weak and beggarly elements, whereunto ye desire again to be in bondage?" 4:10 "Ye observe days, and months, and times, and years." Romans 14:5 "One man esteeneth one day above another: another esteemeth everyday alike. Let every man be fully persuaded in his own mind" Colossians 2:16 "Let no man judge you in meat, or drink, or in respect of an holyday, or of the new moon, or of the sabbath days"*). Let me put it this way. What if a person or church administered Communion on Thursday; the day Jesus actually instituted Communion? Will God condemn them? Or what about on Friday; the day Jesus literally gave up his body and shed his blood? Would that hurt God's feelings, too? There is no scriptural passage in the Bible that directly designates a specific day or condemns any other days involving the *Lord's Supper*.

This biblical example to administer Communion on Sunday is a non-binding example to follow, just as the example to remain single rather than to marry is non-binding when it comes to patterning our lives on the *Apostle Paul*. (*1 Corinthians 7:1 ". . . it is good for a man not to touch a woman" 7:7 "For I would that all men were even as I myself . . ." 7:8 ". . . it is good for them if they abide even as I."*) How should we judge? Should we now condemn all married couples because *Paul* left an example of remaining single? God forbid! And what about when Jesus washed the disciples' feet? (*John 13:14 "If then, your Lord and Master, have washed your feet; ye also ought to wash one another's feet" 13:15 "For I have given you an example, that ye should do as I have done to you."*) Again, shall we judge everyone guilty who has not followed this example by washing their Christian brothers' and sisters' feet? Are there any scriptures that disclose the disciples literally washing feet?

Peter was granted by Jesus the keys of heaven, and that whatever he judged to be righteous on earth, would be judged to be righteous in heaven. (*Matt. 16:19 "And I will give unto thee the keys of the kingdom of heaven: and whatsoever thou shalt bind on earth shall be bound in heaven: and whatsoever shall be loose on earth shall be loosed in heaven.")*

This passage does not insinuate that whatever *Peter* supports on earth will be supported in heaven. *Peter* may advocate marriage or fathering many sons on earth, but these events will never take place in heaven. *Peter* may even support mourning and attending a funeral service of a close relative. But again, these events will never exist inside the gates of heaven. What Jesus is exposing to *Peter* is the things that his faith allows him to do in his heart on earth without condemnation, will be the things that heaven will rule as acceptable also. And the things that his faith convicts him in his heart on earth, will be the things that heaven finds him guilty of as well.

Whatever *Peter* bounded or loosened on earth pertained only to himself, not to every human being. If what *Peter* bounded or loosened on earth decided someone's guilt or innocence, then *Paul* would not have been justified in reprimanding him in Antioch. (*Galatians 2:11 "But when Peter was come to Antioch, I withstood him to the face . . ." 2:14 "But when I saw that they walked not uprightly according to the truth of the gospel, I said unto Peter before them all . . ."*) *Peter* could've easily rebutted *Paul's* condemnation through the position and authority Jesus granted him before his ascension; if this is what the circumstance meant. But it didn't, and the truth is that each Christian will be judged by the faith of himself, not on the faith and beliefs of someone else.

If we are going to condemn congregations or individuals for administering the *Lord's Supper* on days other than the first day of the week, we would have to start with eliminating *Jesus'* statement that represents 'choice-of-time' over 'choice-of-day'. (*1 Corinthians 11:25 ". . . this cup is the new testament in my blood: this ye do, as oft as ye drink it, in remembrance of me."*) It's obvious that Jesus knew days, months, and times. He talked about spending three days in the earth as *Jonah* spent three days in the whale. (*Matt. 12:40 "For as Jonas was three days and three nights in the whale's belly; so shall the Son of man be three days and three nights in the heart of the earth."*) He even foretold the times in which the world would end. (*Matt. 24:14 "And this gospel of the kingdom shall be preached in all the world for a witness unto all nations; and then shall the end come."*)

If Jesus possessed the personality of being thorough and punctual on other significant matters, why would he leave an untimely ritual to be calendared by a church body filled with division, especially when the ritual is designed to immortalize his death until he returns? For Jesus' emphasis was not at all on the timing of Communion, but on what the bread and wine represented, and how the ritual would remind petitioners each session of what he so greatly accomplished on the cross. (*John 3:17 "For God sent not his Son into the world to condemn the world, but that the world through him might be saved."*)

Woman Ministers Approved or Disapproved

I imagine if there were the choice of any scriptural passages that could be forever removed from the Bible by our Christian sisters, they would be, *"Wives submit to your own husbands"* and *"Let the women learn in silence with all subjection."* If any sister doesn't know where to locate these verses in the Bible, just ask a brother and he'll instantly guide you to them. The above topic is another brick set in the wall that divides 'Bible Study' classes farther and farther apart each reviewing.

Throughout regions of the world women have gained tremendous respect for being monumental leaders among their communities, states, and nations. There have been laws passed to sincerely advocate equal rights for women in our society. However, there still remains a dark shadow with a level of abomination that condemns women who stand in the pulpit on Saturday or Sunday morning and preach the gospel. Obviously, not all church affiliations prevent women from preaching, and proudly embrace the idea of having a female leader.

Why do some Christians continue to take offense with women ministers even if their sermon is good, correct, uplifting and edifying? After all, isn't this one of the problems Jesus faced when people judged his person over the message he preached? (*Mark 6:3 "Is not this the carpenter, the son of Mary, the brother of James, and Joses, and Judah, and Simon? Are not his sisters here with us? And they were offended of him."*) Sadly, we too frequently judge the *messenger* over the *message* itself.

How did all the confidence develop for women ministers to preach the gospel on street corners, in auditoriums, and in pulpits arrive? And where does the justification come from to condemn them? Is it only the men who are condemning women ministers or everyone? Although women have broken the barrier in many facets, why hasn't society gotten past the sneering of lady preachers?

Aren't there multitudes of women in the Bible who committed good and noble acts? Didn't God create woman to be man's helpmate? Are not women privileged as the men also to enter into the church building and pray, sing, contribute offerings, and worship God as well? Still, even though some women may be more academically educated, Bible-familiar, and better speakers than their male predecessors, they continue to be strongly opposed if they desire to preach a gospel sermon.

Did the religious community just start this attitude of forbidding women to preach the gospel, or was it passed down through generations? Are there really passages that denounce women evangelists in the Bible? Could there be passages that possibly advocate women evangelists so much 'til some of them even profess that God called them to teach or preach?

Paul's first letter of instruction to *'Timothy'* included rules and regulations that did not support women who dressed too risqué, or for them to teach or have authority over men. (*1 Timothy 2:9 "In like manner also, that women adorn themselves in modest apparel . . ." 2:11 "Let the women learn in silence and all subjection" 2:12 "But I suffer not a woman to teach, nor to usurp authority over the man, but to be in silence.")* Although this piece of manuscript is widely accepted by many church affiliations and is sternly practiced during worship service, it is almost ignored unanimously when it pertains to 'Bible Study' and 'Non-Adult Bible Classes'.

Yes, there are some church establishments that uphold a portion of '*1 Timothy*,' but lack thoroughly maintaining *Paul's* program by designating women to teach, and granting them authority over coed pupils. And most of these churches also allow open comments from women during Bible Study. Others attempt to avoid this allegation by providing classrooms that women oversee outside of the worship center or sanctuary. If any establishment is going to use *Paul's* letter to *'Timothy'* as a guide for church protocol, then it has to be applied according to the 'fine' print as well as the 'bold' print.

When *Paul* made the statement of, *"Let the women learn in silence,"* obviously, this did not mean they couldn't weep, contain their children, sing songs, make confessions or praise God in the house of worship. If he did, he would've had to disclose an alternative program that would accommodate these circumstances. Otherwise worship service would've had very little attraction or purpose for women to attend.

But on the other side of the table sits a congregation who cherishes the belief that a woman has authority to teach the word of God in places other than her home. There are several key verses in the Bible that may play a role in supporting such Christians. One passage includes God revealing his plan to *Jeremiah* for women in the future. (*Jeremiah 31:22 ". . . for the Lord hath created a new thing in the earth, A woman shall compass a man."*) Notice the passage said, "The Lord hath created," not woman. Other scriptural passages women evangelists feed off are: (*Joel 2:28 "And it shall come to pass afterward, that I will pour out my spirit upon all flesh; and your sons and your daughters shall prophesy . . .",*), and of course (*Galatians 3:28 "There is neither Jew nor Greek, there is neither bond nor free, there is neither male or female: for ye are all one in Christ Jesus"*).

It seems the way *Paul* understands it—in the natural world there are distinctions between Jews and Gentiles, males and females. That is how he decides who receives his teachings, along with determining which gender is allowed to preach the gospel. But *Paul* also understands that in the supernatural world there are no distinctions between Jew and Gentile, male or female. One identity fits all. When are Christians supposed to apply *mortal* specifications, and when are Christians not supposed to apply *immortal* specifications is the question that frustrates our religious communities. In this case some church affiliations are sticking with honoring *Paul's* first letter to '*Timothy'* as their guideline to disallow women evangelists from preaching in their establishment, while other affiliations embrace *Paul's* letter to the '*Galatians'* of promoting everyone as being equal through Christ Jesus.

Even though in *Paul's* first letter to *'Timothy'* he specifically forbids women to teach in worship meetings, he still recognizes the churches of God and Jewish custom that allows women to pray and prophesy in public with their heads covered. (*1 Corinthians 11:16 "But if any man seem to be contentious, we have no such custom, neither the churches of God"*)

Well, what did this custom include? (*1 Corinthians 11:4 "Every man praying or prophesying, having his head covered, dishonoureth his head" 11: 5 "But every woman that prayeth or prophesieth with her head uncovered dishonoureth her head . . ." 11:13 "Judge in yourselves: is it comely that a woman pray unto God uncovered?"*) We read in these passages that, obviously, men were allowed to pray and prophesy in public, with the stipulation of not covering their heads. Obviously, women also were allowed to pray and prophesy in public, but with the stipulation of making sure their heads were covered.

Ironic, isn't it? My speculation is; that in the beginning, Jewish custom allowed women to publically pray and prophesy during worship, but *Paul* foresaw some of the future problems which could arise from this tradition; and since this activity was customary rather than law, implemented his attitude as being the better program. (*1 Timothy 2:12 "But I suffer not a woman . . ."*) Not the Lord.

++ Since God is identified as the Father, and Jesus as the Son, and the Holy Spirit as a him, I am more comfortable with men being the governed authority in the church. Also being that Adam was created first, and all of the angels mentioned in the Bible have masculine identities, again, this is my personal reason for desiring a male pastor or preacher to be the leader in the church. However, this does not mean that I believe a male evangelist will receive greater revelation of God's word over a female evangelist. Through my own acquaintances, and by watching several television ministries, women have very much helped to enlighten my understanding of God's word. And although I choose not to be a member of a church institution where a female pastor reigns over the establishment, I will respectively attend any home, seminar, revival, or facility where a female evangelist is faithfully ministering the gospel of Jesus Christ. Remember what *Paul* said to the *Corinthians*: (*1 Corinthians 3:7 "So then neither is he that planteth anything, neither he that watereth; but God that giveth the increase"*).

Miracle Healings and Speaking in Strange Tongues Today

This topic is so conflicting that even many Christians who attend worship services that believe, preach, and practice these behaviors, still hold to a hint of doubt when it comes to accepting it as genuine. Although for a long time man has been astonished by miracles, his timid reservation of the authenticity continues to hinder an immediate acceptance. With today's recording devices, eyewitness accounts and sworn testimonies, why would any church, preacher, or Christian argue against scenarios that represent these events as being active in the 21st century?

The expression 'miracle' is used so loosely today that it's almost common speech. Just ask any sports broadcaster for his transcript and you'll read where he uses the word 'miracle' over and over to categorize last-minute victories. Most college students toss the word 'miracle' around on campus at the disclosure of barely passing semester examines, and combat war vets use no other terminology that explains their surprised survival. Why does the secular world have a passive attitude about 'miracles', while Christians and church affiliations take the term extremely personal?

Not limited to the religious world, but within the entire universe the term 'miracle' in my words mean divine intervention. In some situations it may cause a person or group to highly succeed, yet at the same time cause another person or group to dramatically fail. Whatever the case may be—everyone agrees that the circumstance would not have happened without the act of a miracle.

The Bible documents its first phase of miracles with (*Genesis 1:1 "In the beginning God created the heaven and the earth"*). Which no other being or method could've produced that result. And one of the last miracle recordings to take place is Jesus' proclamation. (*Revelation 22:20 ". . . surely I come quickly . . ."*) Between these two books are countless miracles mostly performed by godly people. However, Christians are predominantly familiar with the miracles introduced by God's prophets, Jesus, and the apostles. Without going into the array of miracles performed throughout the Bible, let's examine some of the ways in which miracles occurred.

All miracles are produced and supervised by the authority of God. Some are performed solely by him (*Genesis 2:21 "And the Lord God caused a deep sleep to fall upon Adam, and he slept; and he took one of his ribs, and closed up the flesh instead thereof" 2:22 "And the rib, which the Lord God had taken from man, made he a woman, and brought her unto man"*), and some are administered by angels (*2 Samuel 24:16 "And when the angel stretched out his hand upon Jerusalem to destroy it, the Lord repented him of the evil . . ." 24:17 "And David spake unto the Lord when he saw the angel that smote the people . . ."*), while other methods included men as the instruments to perform them. (*Acts 5:12 "And by the hands of the apostles were many signs and wonders wrought among the people . . ."*)

Even though there's proof in the Bible that God used human beings to perform miracles, it does not automatically reassure today's Christians that mankind continues to possess this special gift. There are many testimonies of terminally-ill people and cancerous individuals, who have X-rays showing tumors and diseases housed in parts of their bodies. But after personal prayer or prayer from others, final X-rays reveal non-surgical removals of their illnesses. What is so baffling about a minister today who lays hands on a cripple person and then commands that individual, "Stand up and walk," to be viewed as pure fraudulent?

We know certain types of miracles were performed through man for centuries, but what truly seems to be pushing churches farther away from each other mostly regarding miracles, is man's credibility of actually performing the deed.

65

We're going to examine the Scriptures and select passages that promote the ability to miraculously heal people in our era, and then locate other passages that describe those days as being extinct for a human being to perform signs and wonders.

The intimate things Jesus did with his disciples included the confessing of being God's Son, explaining parables, and prophesying events of the future. One of those future events pertained to certain abilities of people that believed on him. (*John 14:11 "Believe me that I am in the Father, and the Father in me: or else believe me for the very works' sake" 14:12 "Verily, verily, I say unto you, He that believeth on me, the works that I do shall he do also; and greater works than these shall he do; because I go unto my Father" 14:13 "And whatsoever ye shall ask in my name, that will I do . . ."*) Jesus not only states that believers would do similar miracles as he did, but they would surpass him, too.

We read another passage where Jesus appeared unto his eleven disciples, this time after his resurrection, and revealed again certain abilities that would follow people that believed on him. (*Mark 16:15 "And he said unto them, 'Go ye into all the world, and preach the gospel to every creature'" 16:16 "He that believeth and is baptized shall be saved . . ." 16:17 "And these signs shall follow them that believe . . ." 16:18 ". . . they shall lay hands on the sick, and they shall recover"*)

Both times when Jesus prepares to leave earth he discusses the signs and wonders that would follow believers—meaning these events would only take place after the Holy Spirit came. Because even though people already believed and were baptized, signs and wonders were not yet implemented to any of them except for his disciples. The eleven elite knew Jesus wasn't just referring to them only when he said, "He that believeth." For they knew Jesus was including everyone who believed in him, and this time there would be no grounds for them to oppose Christians who used Jesus' name to cast out demons and heal people by laying on of hands. We can read in the book of *'Acts'* how the apostles initiated this spiritual gift.

In fact, spiritual gifts became such a craving for believers that *Paul* needed to address the issue with the *Corinthians*. He explained to them where the gifts came from, along with their purposes and identities. (*1*

Corinthians 12:1 "Now concerning spiritual gifts, brethren, I would not have you ignorant" 12:4 "Now there are diversities of gifts but the same Spirit" 12:7 "But the manifestation of the Spirit is given to every man to profit withal" 12:9 "To another faith by the same Spirit; to another the gifts of healing by the same Spirit.")

Still, even if one person had a real desire, opportunity, and empowerment through the Holy Spirit, a distressed individual could easily forfeit his chance of a miraculous healing if his faith didn't commit wholeheartedly. Jesus placed great emphasis and responsibility on recipients who desired a miraculous healing from him. Healing was based on their faith. *(Matt. 9:28 ". . . and Jesus saith unto them, 'Believe ye that I am able to do this?'" 9:29 ". . . according to your faith be it unto you" Luke 17:19 "And he said unto him, 'Arise, go thy way: thy faith hath made you whole.'")*

This required element was a main ingredient the apostles lacked in one case during an attempt to heal a young boy. *(Matt. 17:16 "And I brought him to thy disciples, and they could not cure him" 17:19 "Then came the disciples to Jesus apart, and said, 'Why could not we cast him out?'" 17:20 "And Jesus said unto them, 'Because of your unbelief: for verily I say unto you, if ye have faith as a grain of mustard seed . . . and nothing shall be impossible unto you'" 17:21 "Howbeit this kind goeth not out but by prayers and fasting.")* The book of *'Hebrews'* backs Jesus' attitude: *(Hebrews 11:6 "But without faith it is impossible to please him . . .")*. This passage compels me to trust that it takes a collaboration of faith between all parties in order for the miraculous healing to happen. It has nothing to do with God wanting to heal, his permission, or the era, but with a lacking of faith somewhere that prevents the endeavor from succeeding.

By now we should've established an agreement that the Bible proves God did use people to miraculously heal other individuals, and that it was the Holy Spirit who initially administered supernatural abilities. Plus we know the level of faith between both parties was essential to the success or failure of it. These divine gifts were bestowed upon people who believed in the gospel of Jesus Christ. However, there are many skeptics and church affiliations today who feel they have a legitimate reason for denouncing any shred of evidence that professes miraculous healings to still occur in our time.

In order for me to explain, describe and reason with the skeptics' belief on this matter, I may revert to several previous passages to assist us throughout the discussion. When Christians, preachers or churches deny the possibility of loyal, sincere, God-fearing, obedient followers of Christ who currently possess (or know someone who possesses) the ability to miraculously heal another individual, you can be sure they'll rely on five passages to strongly refute any aspect of confirmation.

These are the most commonly and frequently used passages by the skeptic in denouncing miraculous healings today: (*Acts 19:6 "And when Paul had laid his hands upon them, the Holy Ghost came on them, and they spake with tongues, and prophesied" 6:6 ". . . and when they had prayed, they laid their hands on them" 5:12 "And by the hands of the apostles were many signs and wonders wrought among the people . . ." 2 Corinthians 12:12 "Truly the signs of an apostle were wrought among you in all patience, in signs, and wonders, and mighty deeds" Romans 1:11 "For I long to see you, that I may impart unto you some spiritual gift . . .").* These verses represent three understandings: 'A'—After Jesus ascended to heaven (with the exception of the 'Day-of-Pentecost'), a believer received the Holy Spirit only through the laying on of hands from the apostles. 'B'—The only qualified people who possessed this special privilege, were now dead. 'C'—These twelve mediators were the only people qualified to decide who got the gifts.

Some affiliations stand firmly behind this proclamation, but have no biblical recordings that support their theory on a level they desire. They teach certain attributes from the Holy Spirit ceased once the last apostle died or whom they laid hands upon. None of the Apostles made that claim or taught such message. The Bible states that the *Holy Spirit* granted the gifts to whomever *he* wished, not only the disciples. (*1 Corinthians 12:4 "Now there are diversities of gifts, but the same Spirit" 12:11 "But all these worketh that one the selfsame Spirit, dividing to every man severally as he will."*)

Yes, *Paul* informs believers in the book of *'1 Corinthians'* that the time is coming when specific worldly characteristics will eventually vanish.

"WE'RE RIGHT and THEY'RE WRONG!" A COMMON CHURCH DISEASE

But he never said this adjustment would take place after all the apostles have been laid to rest, or the one's they've laid hands on either.

Also, if miraculous healings have ceased, why would *James* inform Christians to combat illnesses with prayers from the righteous, along with anointing the sick with oil? (*James 5:14 "Is any sick among you? let him call the elders of the church; and let them pray over him, anointing him with oil in the name of the Lord" 5:15 "And the prayer of faith shall save the sick, and the Lord shall raise him up . . ." 5:16 ". . . the effectual fervent prayer of a righteous man availeth much."*) Wouldn't that be a waste of time according to some doctrinal teachings? Or how can an elder help a sick person if he believes otherwise, especially if the person is unconscious and his faith lays dormant?

But two of the greatest passages the skeptic uses in order to denounce miracle healings today are: 'A'—(*1 Corinthians 13:10 "But when that which is perfect is come, then that which is in part shall be done away*). Which *Paul* later explains in *Ephesians 1:9-10 "Having made known unto us the mystery of his will, according to his good pleasure which he hath purposed in himself: That in the dispensation of the fullness of times he might gather together in one all things in Christ, both which are in heaven, and which are on earth."* (This is the true revelation of *1 Cor 13:10* by the same author of the Corinthian book) *1 Corinthians 13:10* combined with *Ephesians 1:9-10* clearly represents a 'perfect time' for God to gather his people to himself, and change the *temporary* relationship a believer has on earth with Him into an *eternal* one in heaven. One part of the prophecy refers to a 'time' circumstance, while the other part refers to a 'completion' and 'upgrading' of the relationship.

'B'—(*1 Corinthians 13:8 ". . . but whether there be prophecies, they shall fail, whether be tongues, they shall cease, whether there be knowledge, it shall vanish away"*) *Prophesies* will no longer be needed because proclamations will have been fulfilled. *Strange tongues* will have ceased also since unbelievers will no longer need them as a sign to prove God exists, and *knowledge* believers now possess will have vanished because a new knowledge will be introduced to them. (*Revelation 21:3 "And I heard a great voice out of heaven saying, 'Behold, the tabernacle of God is with men, and he dwell with them' . . ." 21:4 "And God shall wipe away all tears from their eyes; and there shall be no more death, neither sorrow, nor crying, neither shall there be any more pain: for the former things are passed away" 21:5 "And he who sat upon the throne said, 'Behold, I make all things new' . . .")*

Although the skeptic's understanding and interpretation may promote confidence in denouncing miraculous healings today, one overlooked revelation may lie in a nearby verse. (*1 Corinthians 13:9 "For we know in part, and we prophesy in part"*) What do we know in part, and what are we prophesying in part?

What we **'know in part'** pertains to our knowledge of spiritual principalities: their positions, capabilities, duties, and relationships toward God, as well as the complete role Christians will have in serving him. And what we **'prophesy in part'** pertains to our limited ability to understanding how everything will unfold as it develops into a united universe who loves and worships one God forever. (*John 3:11 "Verily, verily, I say unto thee, 'We speak that we do know, and testify that we have seen; and you receive not our witness'" 3:12 "If I have told you earthly things, and ye believe not, how shall ye believe, if I tell you of heavenly things?'" John 16:12 "I have yet many things to say unto you, but ye cannot bear them now."*) This means we know in part because we're creatures of the *natural world*. Even *Paul* admits his own lacking of spiritual comprehension (*1 Cor 13:12 ". . . I know in part . . ."*), and complete understanding will come from the *supernatural world* in God's timing.

So, *"that which is perfect is come,"* will only come when God receives from his entire creation what he desires and deserves, and *"that which is in part shall be done away"* will only happen after God has wiped the believers' tears for good and has given them an incorruptible crown. (*Rev. 7:17 ". . . and God shall wipe away all tears from their eyes" James 1:12 "Blessed is the man that endureth temptation: for when he is tried, he shall receive the crown of life, which the Lord hath promised to them that love him"*)

Even though the same enthusiasm and principles may encourage attitudes against 'speaking in strange tongues', there are a few passages that might reveal something startling to skeptics. Obviously, the *'Corinthian'* believers wrote *Paul* about things they were divided over, and *Paul* was concerned enough to write them a long letter in response. Unfortunately, we too, are struggling today with the same questions that surround gifts of the Holy Spirit, which *Paul* candidly answers. (*1 Corinthians 12:1 "Now concerning spiritual gifts, brethren, . . ." 12:7 "But the manifestation of the Spirit is given to every man to profit withal"*)

One testimony that rules out only twelve men possessing this 'gift' and whoever they lay hands on; is that *the Spirit is given to every man*, and if the 'Spirit' is given to every man, how could the 'gifts' not be given to every man? Especially, when just four passages further ahead *'1 Corinthians 12:11'* reads: *"But all these worketh that one and the selfsame Spirit, dividing to every man severally as he will."* Again, the presentation of *'every man'* is specified, not only to Jesus' hand-picked twelve apostles and whoever they've touched. And out of nine spiritual gifts that are mentioned, two gifts *Paul* refers to are spoken about in this same chapter. (*1 Corinthians 12:8 "For to one is given by the Spirit the word of wisdom . . ." 12:9 "To another faith by the same Spirit; to another the gifts of healing by the same Spirit" . . . 12:10 ". . . to another divers kinds of tongues; to another the interpretation of tongues"*)

Paul uses an analogy of the human body to explain the diverse parts, functions, and purpose of spiritual gifts. These members unify believers as a whole, rather than separating them into a group that looks down on each other or think one gift is more important. (*1 Corinthians 12:12 "For as the body is one, and hath many members, and all the members of that one body, being many, are one body: so also is Christ" 12:14 "For the body is not one member, but many."*)

Paul continues to emphasize the importance of believers respecting every spiritual gift. (*1 Corinthians 12:15 "If the foot shall say, 'Because I am not the hand, I am not of the body; is it therefore not of the body?'" 12:16 "And if the ear shall say, 'Because I am not the eye, I am not of the body; is it therefore not of the body?'"*) Plus, *Paul* reminds us that it's God who designs the body for his purpose, not for man's purposes. (*1 Corinthians 12:18 "But now hath God set the members every one of them in the body, as it hath pleased him" "Romans 9:21 "Hath not the potter power over the clay . . ."*)

In *Paul's* conclusion he demands respect and unity from Christians toward the gifts of the Holy Spirit, whether they are plain or extravagant. (*1 Corinthians 12 :21 "And the eye cannot say unto the hand, 'I have no need of thee,' nor again the head to the feet, I have no need of you'" 12:23 "And those members of the body, which we think to be less honorable, upon these we bestow more abundant honor . . ."*)

And finally *Paul* speaks about the order in which God has placed his attributes to be categorized. (*1 Corinthians 12:28 "And God hath set some in the church, first apostles, secondarily prophets, thirdly teachers, after that miracles, then gifts of healings, helps, government, diversities of tongues."*) This passage starts off by informing its readers that God has rightfully chosen to setup 'some' in the church, not all, with these titles and abilities. (*1 Corinthians 12:29 "Are all apostles? Are all prophets? Are all workers of miracles?" 12:30 "Have all the gifts of healing? Do all speak with tongues? Do all interpret?"*) If there was every an opportunity for *Paul* to inform Christians that the spiritual gift of 'speaking in strange tongues' is going to cease immediately after the last apostle's death or who they've touched, this would be the ideal epistle, chapter and topic to validate such claim.

On the contrary, *Paul* continues to uphold 'speaking in strange tongues'. (*1 Corinthians 13:8 ". . . whether there be tongues, they shall cease . . ."*). He still contributes an entire chapter with nearly five hundred more words surrounding 'speaking in strange tongues,' to his already lengthy letter. *Paul's* final advice to the *'Corinthian '* church in Chapter Fourteen is for them to not suppress the 'speaking of strange tongues' during worship service. (*1 Corinthians 14:39 "Wherefore, brethren, covet to prophesy, and forbid not to speak with tongues."*) What *Paul* is attempting to teach the Corinthians, and us, in *1 Corinthians Chapter 13* is that no one needs to get caught up in who possesses the gifts of speaking in 'strange tongues' or who heals or who gives his body to be burned. Because in due time all of these aspects will have lost their luster; and the only talent that's going to hold up in the court of Christian service is LOVE. Jesus told his disciples a similar message in *Luke 10:19-20 "Don't rejoice that the demons are subject to you (a spiritual gift), but be rather glad because your names are written in heaven."* Both in authority are telling their listeners to concentrate on the most important issue that will matter in the end, rather than crave or glory in a supernatural ability right now.

Even though this cluster of affirmation may be sufficient for most believers, some believers still maintain lasting skepticism due to the interpretation of a few final passages. (*1 Corinthians 14:22 "Wherefore tongues are for a sign, not to the believer, but to them that believe not . . ." 14:23 ". . . and all speak with tongues, and there come in those that are unlearned, or unbelievers, will they not say that ye are mad?"*)

If one agrees with *Paul's* proclamation that the purpose of 'speaking in tongues' is one of the great signs to help convert unbelievers, then why would this 'faith-changing' method be abruptly dropped? Obviously, there are even more unbelievers in the world now than 2000 years ago. Has the number of believers been fulfilled? Did we skip a page? One part of the passage reads, "Not to them that believe, but to them that believe not" (*". . . but prophesying serveth not for them that believe not, but for them which believe" 1 Cor. 14:22*).

Yes, the passage is a two-part illustration. For the **unbeliever**—hearing Christians *'speaking in strange tongues'* is considered proof. For the **believer**—*'prophesying'* or proclaiming God's word is considered proof unto you. If both unbeliever and believer are going to remain in this body, on this earth until Christ returns (*Matt. 13:30 "Let both grow together until the harvest . . ." Matt. 26:11 "For you have the poor always with you . . ."*), then how can one confirmation cease and the other remain? They go hand-in-hand with the purpose of convincing and convicting witnesses while in their current faith. There has not been a separation between the unbeliever and believer yet, and there won't be until the end of time. And if no separation has occurred, then no ceasing of signs and prophesies has either.

Still, in an attempt to remain loyal to a longtime misrepresentation, many skeptics condemn affiliations who advocate 'speaking in strange tongues' during worship service because its presentation sometimes opposes *Paul's* instructions concerning proper conduct. (*1 Corinthians 14:27 "If any man speak in an unknown tongue, let it be by two or at the most three, and that by course, and let one interpret" 14:28 "But if there be no interpreter, let him keep silence in the church, and let him speak to himself, and to God"*)

While it's true that many skeptics can rightfully accuse some Christians of disobeying *Paul's* instruction on 'conduct' concerning how to 'speak in strange tongues', this accusation carries no merit when pleading to deny its existence. You cannot say just because the driver of a car didn't apply the road rules and then wrecked, that since he didn't follow the instructions, society can also denounce the car from ever existing. Can you? No, the car would still exist apart from the driver breaking the road rules.

++ I would not credit or discredit any individual that he's 'speaking in strange tongues' because I didn't understand what he said while praising God. Neither do I judge any miraculous healing. I currently do not possess the authority or ability to decide either situation. The only thing that believers can frown upon is that there are some Christians who are breaking biblical road rules about 'speaking in strange tongues.' But only God can write the ticket violation, not us.

Below is part of an email discussion about this topic from another Magazine Author, who took a friend to a revival that had a major extremity injury but came away from it unhealed. The author does not believe in miracle healing today and claim he's proved its falsehood.

me: Although I do agree with you when you say in your article that there are miracle deceivers in the religious community, and that Jesus performed miracles that were unmatched before and during his missionary, I cannot fully support your claim of miracles do not exist any longer today based on your Scriptural interpretation alone. I know you took your friend to the revival to be healed, but did your friend's faith let her down. Did you bring her to test God? We know outside of God's power, faith is as important as power. Jesus said, *"If you had faith the size of a mustard seed . . ."* How many times did Jesus ask the needy, *". . . do you believe I can heal you?"* and *". . . your faith has made you whole."*

MA: I did not take my friend to the revival to test God. I took her to test the claims of false teachers/healers. They promised to heal anyone who would come. I wanted to (and did) expose their fraud. As to faith, sometimes miracles were performed on people without faith. Jesus raised the dead son of a widow (*Luke 7:11-15*), and Paul struck Elymas, an enemy of all righteousness, blind (*Acts 13:8-11*). If it is a question of faith, at least in these two cases, it had nothing to do with the faith of the man being healed.

me: So you did take your friend to the revival with the ulterior motive to test first, regardless of who, rather than the healing itself? Was your revival visit more-so aimed at proving an authenticity over receiving the healing for your friend? How far was the revival's drive? Did you and your friend have lots of time to discuss and anticipate the endeavor on a negative note? Is your friend a supporter or member of your church doctrine? Surely you wouldn't escort someone to a healing revival whose doctrine contradicts your belief? So did the revival have two doubters to begin with? *Mark 11:23 ". . . and shall not doubt in his heart . . ."* Plus *James* warns us *"that no one who doubts is to expect to receive anything from God."* I am not saying that you did not expose someone fraudulent, because the Bible has already warned us about false teachers. I am saying if this initial attitude and tactic about experiencing miracles is going to be your cornerstone, why should God show you a big miracle when you doubt even the smallest? If faith the size of a mustard seed can move mountains, how much smaller need the seed of doubt be to prevent it?

MA: Yes, my friend and I do agree in the same theology. But you miss the point. I do not question the power of God to perform miracles. I was simply testing false prophets, not God. Back to the Bible passages. There is absolutely no indication that the woman (*Luke 7:11-15)* nor her son knew Jesus or already believed in Him. If Jesus performed this miracle on the woman's dead son without him having faith, why wouldn't He do the same today if it was His will to do so? I believe I am correct with this understanding about the necessity of faith when it pertains to performing miracles.

me: In both biblical cases it was Jesus himself, or a direct order through God that initiated the miracle. But you and I are talking about ordinary people of today, where faith on either side will always be a factor. *"Without faith it is impossible to please God."* I am not saying that you have no faith in God or that you deny his power and abilities. But, instead, that you do not have sufficient enough scriptures to support your interpretation that God no longer uses human beings to perform healing miracles today. And although you may have exposed a false prophet with your experience at the revival, this does not prove to be a global absolute. Do you not believe Jesus in *Mark 16:16?* Of course you do. But why not believe *Mark 16:17-18?* It's just a verse away. Is this a statement or confession by Jesus in the Bible that's only half true?

MA: I do believe all of *Mark 16:16-18.* These verses do not say, however, that these signs would be performed by All Believers for All Time. The passage does not say that every believer would have miraculous power but that signs would accompany the believers. Signs accompanied the apostles and early Christians with spiritual gifts (*Acts 2:43, 5:12, 6:8, 8:5 & 1Cor 12:14*). These signs accompany us today in that we have the written record of the miracles that were performed by the apostles and those with spiritual gifts. Do you take up serpents and drink deadly poison without ill effects today? Why don't the claimants of modern miracles do these things?

me: I know every believer is not a teacher, prophet or apostle. Not everyone has the power to work miracles or to heal or to speak strange tongues *1Cor 12:29-30.* However, we're not focusing on the believers who cannot perform miracles; we're discussing the ones who can. Let us be careful about adding to the Bible based on what it does not say (All Believers for All Time). For this is what many people do with *Ephesians 5:19.* They teach the Bible doesn't SAY don't play musical instruments. I'm sure you've heard that before. And, no, I do not take up serpents and drink deadly poison. *Mark 16:18* simply means during one's journey if he encountered being accidentally bitten by a poison snake (from resting on the ground or from lying on a rock, or climbing a tree), then he would not be harmed. It does not suggest that a believer grabs a known poison snake and show-off or test God with it. And drinking poison and not becoming ill meant if on your journey someone attempts to poison you because of the Gospel, again, you would not be harmed. This passage is not designed for anyone to voluntarily consume known toxins. Evildoers went through great means to silence the Gospel of Christ, and look what they even did to Jesus. He said, *"I am sending you out as sheep among wolves."* Correct me if I'm wrong, but I think the entire belief of *miracles have ceased* mainly arises from one passage in the Bible: *1 Cor 13:10.* In your affiliation's doctrinal belief this verse has the equivalency of the scriptures that claim Christ has risen. If Christ has not died for our sins and has not risen to life, Christians have no hope or doctrine of worthiness. In the same scenario, if *1 Cor 13:10* does not represent *miracles have ceased* today, then where does that put your faith? Or just as important, where does that put your opponent's faith?

MA: You were the one using *Mark 16:16-18* to affirm that believers will perform miraculous signs today. You are the one who's making the passage say more that what it says. I simply pointed out that the passage doesn't promise believers today miraculous powers. The truth is, and I think I said this, signs do follow us today. *"Therefore many other signs Jesus also performed in the presence of the disciples, which were not written in this book; but these have been written so that you may believe that Jesus is the Christ, the Son of God . . ."* (*John 20:30-31*). Signs were given to "confirm the word", and a covenant once confirmed, needs no further confirmation (Gal 3:15).

me: Who is Jesus talking about when he says, *Matt. 7:22 "Many will say to me in that day, Lord, Lord, have we not prophesied in thy name? and in thy name cast out devils, and in thy name done many wonderful works?"* Which Jesus eventually sends them to their destruction? If Jesus is not condemning the Apostles, then who else could be guilty of performing miracles? Or is it safe to say that this is one *sin* that Christians of our era are exempted from since God doesn't allow his Spirit to work miracles through man anymore?

MA: In this passage Jesus condemns the disobedient, period! Perhaps there were people in the first century who had or claim to have possessed miraculous power but who reverted to a lawless life and stood condemned. Most likely Jesus is talking about the Jews who claimed to be able to perform miracles (*Matt 12:27*), but whose claims were false. The *sin* of making false claims by disobedient people is present in every age, but that doesn't prove that people perform miracles today.

me: When Jesus made the claim that, *"Not everyone who says, Lord, Lord, will enter the Kingdom,"* this event was during the end of time gathered around the Judgment Seat. It won't be any guessing or mistakes about who actually performed miracles or casts out demons and who didn't. If Jesus is not referring to the Apostles, he is talking about Christians who believed in him and who preached in his name. And even though they did what they did for the wrong reason, they still performed the miracles. Is this not true?

MA: It's really not my point to deny that lawless people performed genuine miracles. I won't even argue that arguable point with you. But even if they did, that doesn't prove miracles are performed today. The greater works that Jesus was talking about that believers would do were spiritual in nature—leading lost souls into the kingdom. Please not that the apostles would be enabled to do greater works because Jesus was going to the Father. Many things in the spiritual realm that were impossible during Jesus' humiliation were made possible by His exaltation: the forgiveness of sins, the establishment of the church, the conversion of the Gentiles, ect.

me: Why are you attempting to limit the greater works that Jesus said believers would do to just spreading the Gospel, when he's clearly talking about miracle works? And that's when the *Holy* Spirit came anyway—after His exaltation. And forgiveness for sins was already on earth with the baptism of John-the-Baptist, plus Jesus forgave sins during his earthly missionary as well. It was part of the reason he offended the Jews: through his proclamation.

If your theory is true, why does Jesus say, *"That if you believe on me?"* (*John 14:14 "If ye shall ask anything in my name, I will do it"*)? I know just because you ask for a person to become a Christian in the name of Jesus, does not mean that person will become a Christian. So what was Jesus talking about when he assured every believer that he would do for them if they asked in his name, if it wasn't a physical miracle?

Throughout the email conversation the magazine author and I discussed several scriptures that you've already read in the earlier pages concerning *miracles have ceased*, mostly due to *1 Corinthians 13:8-10*. So I won't repeat myself, but get to the conclusion of the discussion.

me: Sir, I cannot explain exactly how faith works totally in the spiritual world and with us. I know it is an element that we are justified by; neither can you please God without it. It is a subject that the 'New Testament' constantly reminds us about, and it's what we're saved by. And even if we don't see who had the most or least faith, somebody has to have it in order for it to work. I have shown you word for word using direct quotes in the Bible that literally say, *"Believers shall do the works I do . . ."* John 14:12 and *"they shall lay hands on the sick and they shall recover"* Mark 16:18. You cannot alter or defeat a direct quotation with an opinion or interpretation. That would be like someone reading the Ten Commandments, *"thou shalt not have no other gods before me,"* and then that person finds other verses in the Bible to help suggest that the passage meant, "as long as God is first, you can have other gods." Interpretations and opinions are too weak to diminish or defuse any direct quote in the Bible. All Bible scholars know there is no biblical passage or verse that quotes Jesus or any Apostle saying that miracles will have ceased at the death of the last apostle, or whom they've laid hands upon, or once you read past *1 Corinthians 13:10.* The only real evidence you have that makes *'miracles have ceased'* today is that you refuse to believe that they have not. If you are going to continue your crusade to prove to millions of people that they are being deceived by their own eyes, faith and experiences, then your up-hill battle is probably going to leave the task incomplete. Unless, perhaps, there comes along a miracle.

PS: Still waiting for email response.

Which Shines Brighter, the Cheerful Giver, or the Person Who Tithes

There are very few books written that advise people how to live a happy, peaceful, and prosperous life without mentioning the stewardship of money, and the Bible is no exception. It doesn't matter if a church institution represents itself as being large or small, denominational or non-denominational, the entire congregation knows the irreplaceable value of a cheerful giver or faithful tither. Unfortunately, some Christians choose their 'place-of-worship' based on the institution's financial rule-of-thumb.

In fact, it wasn't very long during Jesus' ministry that he was setup by the scribes and chief priests who used spies in their effort to trap him with laws concerning money. (*Luke 20:20 ". . . and sent forth spies . . . that they might take hold of his words, that so they might deliver him unto the power and authority of the government."*) These men questioned Jesus in front of many people. (*Luke 20:22 "Is it lawful for us to give tribute unto Caesar, or no?"*) Jesus' reply sets the standard for all men concerning taxes, debts, offerings and tithes. (*Luke 20:25 "And he said unto them, 'Render therefore unto Caesar the things which be Caesar's, and unto God the things which be God's.' "*)

The Jews were aware that ancient Scriptures had already presented a similar case in the Old Testament. (*Malachi 3:8 "Will a man rob God? Yet ye have robbed me . . ." 3:9 "Ye are cursed with a curse: for ye have robbed me, even this whole nation" 3:10 "Bring ye all the tithes into the storehouse . . ."*), and adding to this problem in the extreme were people believing it was more important to give to God's cause first, even if their parents were in destitution. (*Mark 7:11 "But ye say, 'If a man shall say to his father or mother, 'It is Corbin, that is to say, a gift, by whatsoever thou mightest be profited by me; he shall be free.' "*)

Money has been an issue in the religious world as well as in the secular world for a very long time. Even though many Christians agree that giving to the church is an obligation necessary to strengthen and maintain all aspects of its biblical functions, to emphasize cash amounts given by members and non-members can sometime break relationships. There are lots of people who cheerfully deposit their funds into the money trays, while others regulate the contribution by one tenth of their earnings.

Although the issue is not whether one protocol produces more revenue than the other, still, there has to be a reason why some Christians feel guilty when not contributing a specified portion to God. Whereas, other Christians show no regret in giving any amount as long as it's done in good spirits.

Let's see if we can locate a few passages where the initial concept of people giving portions back to God was recognized and accepted as a noble activity. (*Genesis 4:4 "And Able, he also brought of the firstlings of his flock and of the fat thereof. And the Lord had respect unto Able and to his offering."*) Inside this same book we read where another patriarch applies a specific measurement of ten percent offered to show his gratitude towards the king. (*Genesis 14:20 "And blessed be the most high God, which hath delivered thine enemies into thy hand, and he gave him tithes of all."*) We also read in the Scriptures where God delegates a portion of 'ten percent' to the tribe of *Levi* for administering religious services. (*Numbers 18:24 "But the tithes of the children of Israel, which they offer as an heave offering unto the Lord, I have given to the Levites to inherit . . ."*) Plus, we read one passage that addresses an entire nation concerning required provisions to be contributed. (*Deuteronomy 14:22 "Thou shalt truly tithe all the increase of thy seed, that the field bringeth forth year by year."*)

The above verses surely display evidence that promotes the cycle of giving God what belongs to him. These laws were not only common, but were repeatedly demanded from his worshippers. But out of a million items God could've required people to share as a form of obedience, why would he choose only one? And why would that one choice be money when society constantly reminds us that, "Money isn't everything?"

Anyone familiar with the Bible knows by now that the God they've read about certainly requires sacrifice as a main expression of willingness. He wants his worshippers to render certain things at significant levels. (*John 3:16 "For God so loved the world, that he gave his only begotten Son, that whosoever believeth in him should not perish, but have everlasting life."*) God decided that 'money' would be a significant area in which we could express our willingness to not only be pruned and groomed for sharing, but also be a tremendous help for everyone in need.

Since money was introduced to man, he has exhausted every supply of resources in order to acquire more of it than he currently possesses. And even when he obtains an abundance of it, he spends many sleepless nights worrying how to keep others from getting it. (*Ecclesiastes 5:12 ". . . but the abundance of the rich will not suffer him to sleep"*)

Yet, this is the artifact God requires from worshippers when he asks them to contribute an element of worthiness. What's the 'big deal' about giving our hard-earned money to church organizations? Why does it have to be cash? Why couldn't it be another type of means? Why not let it be old clothes, worn tires, junky cars, empty cans or bottles, furniture, shoes, etcetera? We certainly have more than we need of those commodities. The answer is we would never feel the level of commitment, responsibility and humility that comes with releasing money, compared to contributing any other item.

Remember when the rich man boasted of his obedience toward the Ten Commandments and then Jesus told him the ingredient he lacked that kept him from being perfect? (*Luke 18:20 "Thou knowest the commandments . . ." 18:21 ". . . and he said, 'All these I have kept from my youth'" 18:22 "Now when Jesus heard these things, he said unto him, 'Yet lackest thou one thing: sell all that thou hast . . . and follow me.' "*) But someone may still ask, "What does contributing my money to God's cause, whether given cheerfully or by percentage earnings, do for me personally as a Christian?

Working slowly from the outside in, it eventually helps us decide which master we're going to serve: God or money? (*Luke 16:13 "No servant can serve two masters: for either he will hate the one, and love the other; or else he will hold to the one, and despise the other. Ye cannot serve God and mammon."*) While another Christian may say, "Even the world gives you something in return on an investment. What about the monies we invest each weekend at church?"

Needless to say, everyone wants to know if their sacrifices have been appreciated or taken for granted. Surprisingly, a similar question arose from one of the apostles to Jesus. (*Matt. 19:27 "Then answered Peter unto him, 'Behold, we have forsaken all, and followed thee; what shall we have therefore?'" 19:28 "And Jesus said unto them, 'Verily I say unto you, 'That ye which have followed me' . . ." 19:29 ". . . shall receive an hundredfold, and shall inherit everlasting life.' "*) Apart from gaining eternal life, the spiritual growth produced through delegating a portion of money to the religious sector molds your heart into the image of God, who created us. (*Genesis 1:27 "So God created man in his own image, in the image of God created he him . . ."*) God is a committed giver, and he wants us to be generous like himself. (*James 1:5 ". . . that giveth to all men liberally, and upbraideth not . . ." Matt. 7:11 ". . . how much more shall your Father in heaven give good things to them that ask him?"*) For we all know the familiar saying of, "It's better to give than to receive." (*Acts 20:35 ". . . and to remember the words of the Lord Jesus, how he said, 'It is more blessed to give than to receive.' "*)

This is one of those 'character builders' that takes a while for a person to completely understand. It's identical to the cliché: "This is going to hurt me more than you." For most of us this is one 'character builder' that took a long time for us to fully grasp. But eventually we got it and passed it on. The same circumstance applies to principles concerning *giving*.

Plus, God assures us that our contributions will not go unnoticed or unrewarded. (*Proverbs 19:17 "He that have pity upon the poor lendeth unto the Lord; and that which he hath given will he pay him again" Malachi 3:10 "Bring ye all the tithes into the storehouse, that there may be meat in mine house, and prove me now herewith, saith the Lord of hosts, if I will not open you the windows of heaven, and pour you out a blessing, that there shall not be room enough to receive it.")*

But let us make sure we don't misunderstand the true structure of giving by assuming *amount* outweighs *attitude*. On the contrary, Jesus illustrates an excellent example when several rich men contributed their tithes, versus the tiny amount given by a poor widow woman. (*Luke 21:1 "And he looked up, and saw the rich men casting their gifts into the treasury" 21:2 "And he saw also a certain poor widow casting in thither two mites" 21:3 "And he said, 'Of a truth I say unto you, that this poor widow hath cast in more than they all'" 21:4 "For all these have of their abundance cast in unto the offerings of God: but she of her penury hath cast in all the living that she had.")*

In other words; even though the rich men gave much, their generosity was judged as being too superficial or shallow-hearted. Their contributions may have earned merits toward the aid provided to the Temple treasury, but their financial sacrifice had no personal or spiritual impact on them. Whereas, the poor widow's contribution possessed very little aid to the Temple treasury, but had an enormous impact on her personally and spiritually. She gave her all.

This scenario has brought us to the primary question of *which shines brighter?* For the person who tithes, we understand you extracted your inspiration and convictions from the 'Old Testament' standards. But what about the 'Cheerful Givers?' What Scriptural passage or passages in the New Testament could they use to support their beliefs? How about in the book of '2 Corinthians?' (*2 Corinthians 9:7 ". . . so let him give; not grudgingly, or of necessity: for God loveth a cheerful giver" Romans 12:8 ". . . he that giveth, let him do it with simplicity.")*

Does contributing to 'church offerings' in a courteous manner, along with a good attitude, eliminate an individual from being held responsible for donating as much as he actually could? Or perhaps even should? Well, one thing a person has to constantly be aware of is the impact he feels from his/her sacrifice. One of God's chief designs in this world is the law of sacrifice. You cannot get anything in this world unless you give something. Even when a gift is given, you still have to sacrifice your non-refundable time in order to receive it.

Apart from the commanded ten percent established in the 'Old Testament' in order to build revenue for payment to the *Levites* and other religious services, it created a pattern of consistency for the children of Israel. The procedure also subtracted an adequate amount from their earnings that promoted reverence and trust in their personalities toward God.

The emphasis is not so much on 'regulated-type' offerings or 'dollar amount' contributions, but more on the effect and impact a person's gift has on himself. Does he feel, if not contributing by the standard ten percent, that his sacrificial portion is a worthy amount compared to what God has already blessed him with—regardless whether simplicity and high spirits are attached to it?

++ While ten percent of a person's gross earnings is the uniformed policy that implements a simple guideline for setting aside money during church offerings, it hardly excuses anyone who contributes with a grumpy or arrogant attitude. All monies should be given with a spirit of willingness, humility, and confidence.

In the end the person who *tithes* should not judge the person who *cheerfully gives*. Likewise, the person who *cheerfully* gives should not judge the person who *tithes*. I, personally, attempt to do my best in tithing, but sometimes, not very often, I cheerfully give; and that's still a dollar amount I try to feel in my spirit as well as in aiding the treasury. (*Luke 6:38 ". . . For with the same measure that ye mete withal it shall be measured to you again."*)

Does it matter what day a church assigns for the receiving of tithes and offerings? I won't get into that, but if you want an example to follow, look up the passage in '1 Corinthians: Chapter 16.' One of *Paul's* main agendas is to keep 'church order' during worship meetings while still leaving some protocols to the decisions of the establishment. What day an institution collects its gifts from the congregation may or may not be one of those decisions.

How are we Born Again and What does it Mean

Even though this is a topic that all church affiliations agree upon concerning a Christian's mandatory experience in order to enter into the Kingdom, the methods that are used to determine how we're Born Again puts them right back in the war zone. When I pursued a citywide church survey pertaining to the theology that affiliations were divided over, one of the key questions asked inside the pamphlet was: "What must a person do to be saved?" Only 1 church institution out of 25 literally answered, "Be Born Again."

It's ironic that even today's religious leaders are still pondering what it means to be Born Again, and how we're born of water and of the Spirit. In fact, it wasn't too long ago that I heard a sermon on the topic of being Born Again; and it started out something like this: "Scholars say that wise men did not travel the streets of Jerusalem after dark because many dangers blotted the narrow streets and darkened doorways. It would usually take an emergency or important mission to compel a man to wander the pathways during those ancient times." Which the preacher was referring to Nicodemus' mission to find and talk to Jesus alone one night.

It is at this point in the book of *John* where we read who Nicodemus was identified as (*John 3:1 "There was a man of the Pharisees, named Nicodemus, a ruler of the Jews"*). Now it is safe to say that Nicodemus either knew where Jesus was located or had searched diligently in order to find him. We don't know if Nicodemus broke his curfew, left the Pharisees meeting to question Jesus about Temple issues that occurred just hours earlier, or played hooky. But we do know from the earlier description of the dangers surrounding someone being out on the streets alone: obviously meant Nicodemus was desperate. And from the way the Bible records Nicodemus' and Jesus' opening conversation, Nicodemus immediately acknowledges and compliments Jesus on his authority and deeds, (*John 3:2 ". . . and said unto him, Rabbi, we know that thou art a teacher come from God: for no man can do these miracles that thou doest, except God be with him "*). Here we have a highly religious leader of the chosen nation consider Jesus enough to include him in his busy, religious/political day, elude the dangers to find Jesus, and then open the conversation on a very civil note. You would think the average person would probably thank the individual for his acknowledgement and kind words before getting to the heart-of-the-matter. Or at least say a few polite words back to them in regards to being familiar with their position as well, right? No, not Jesus.

Jesus' first words back to Nicodemus, almost in the form of a riddle, are words that speak of his jeopardized soul. Undoubtedly a scenario that Nicodemus never expected or heard in his life: (*John 3:3 "Verily, verily, I say unto thee, 'Except a man be born again, he cannot see the kingdom of God' "*). Whatever initial reason Nicodemus had to visit Jesus, I'm sure, just became irrelevant compared to Jesus' proclamation. Yet, Nicodemus, in a concern, but almost sarcastic manner, responds in search of an answer. (*John 3:4 ". . . how can a man be born when he is old? can he enter the second time into his mother's womb, and be born?"*) Jesus attempts to give Nicodemus another angle of this truth by elaborating on the subject: (*John 3:5-6 ". . . Verily, verily, I say unto thee, 'Except a man be born of water and of the Spirit, he cannot enter into the kingdom of God'" "That which is born of flesh is flesh; and that which is born of the Spirit is spirit "*). Realizing Nicodemus was baffled, Jesus then explains what the Spirit and the wind had in common: (*John 3:8 "The wind bloweth where it listeth, and thou hearest the sound thereof, but canst not tell whence it cometh, and whither it goeth: so is every one that is born of the Spirit "*).

Even though Jesus reveals ingredients and metaphors to help Nicodemus understand his statement, Nicodemus responds with nearly identical words of when Jesus first told him about being Born Again (*John 3:9 ". . . how can these things be?"*).

All of the biblical recordings where birth is impossible from a natural standpoint, but possible from a supernatural standpoint, seem to have the same concern to its candidates of *how* could the activity exist? This question dates all the way back to Sarah and Abraham. (*Genesis 18:10 ". . . Sarah thy wife shall have a son . . ."18:11 "Now Abraham and Sarah were old and well stricken in age . . ." 18:12 "Therefore Sarah laughted within herself. . ."*) Next, a priest named Zacharias also had the identical concerns as did Nicodemus when he was told about a peculiar birth, (*Luke 1:13 "But the angel said unto him: 'Fear not, Zacharias; for thy prayer is heard, and thy wife Elisabeth shall bear thee a son . . .'" 1:18 "And Zacharias said unto the angel, 'Whereby shall I know this? for I am an old man, and my wife well stricken in years' "*). And again we see Mary, Jesus' mother, having equal doubt and confusion when the angel Gabriel first told her about her supernatural conception: (*Luke 1:30-31 "And the angel said unto her, 'Fear not, Mary: for thou hast found favor with God.'" "And behold, thou shalt conceive in thy womb, and bring forth a son, and shalt call his name Jesus' "*). Mary then responds like Nicodemus as did the others, (*1:34 "Then said Mary unto the angel, 'How shall this be, seeing that I know not a man' "*). Despite being God's chosen people and most of them knowing many miracles recorded in the 'Books of Israel', they all lacked the main ingredient—*belief*. None of these people remembered or apparently believed that nothing was too hard or impossible for God: *Genesis 18:14 "Is anything too hard for the Lord?" Jeremiah 32:27 "Behold, I am the Lord, the God of all flesh; is there anything too hard for me?"* Jesus himself was a supernatural birth, yet Nicodemus still failed to understand that a man could be Born Again supernaturally with God.

When all of the above patriarchs were inform of a miracle birth coming their way, they were not assigned or instructed to do something physical on their own to activate the process; such as to go on a month's fasting or withdraw to a secluded area or even dip seven times into the Jordan. This is why Jesus, after Nicodemus does not confess him to be the Christ, immediately discusses Nicodemus' problem that's going to keep him from entering the Kingdom: (*John 8:24 "I said therefore unto you, that ye shall die in your sins: for if ye believe not that I am he, ye shall die in your sins"*).

Along with Nicodemus' *tiny* description of Jesus, to Jesus, Jesus knew that the Pharisees did not believe he was the Messiah (*John 7:47-48 "Then answered them the Pharisees, 'Are you also deceived?'" "Have any of the rulers or Pharisees believed on him?" 8:13 "The Pharisees said unto him, Thou bearest record of thyself, thy record is not true"*). I know this was a long walk before arriving at this point, but it was very necessary in order to explain the true meaning or essence of what Jesus meant when he told Nicodemus, *"Except a man be born again, he cannot see the kingdom of God."*

When Jesus says, *"Except a man be born of water,"* Jesus is not referring to H2O as we know it, nor is he comfirming that a person must be baptized. Baptism has many other scriptures in the New Testament that advocate its importance and position in regards to salvation, and did not need to subpoena *John 3:5* as a witness. Plus, Nicodemus, being a Pharisees, was already familiar with baptism (*Matt. 3:1 "In those days came John the Baptist, preaching in the wilderness of Judaea" 3:7 "But when he saw many of the Pharisees and Sadducees come to his baptism . . ."*). Nicodemus could've saved himself a lot of time and embarrassment by solving the spiritual mystery through the mentioning of baptism to Jesus instead of entering his mother's womb. Or Jesus could've easily invited Nicodemus to tomorrow's baptism His disciples were administering in Judaea; if it would've clarified being *born of water* (*John 3:22 "After these things came Jesus and his disciples into the land of Judaea, and there he tarried with them, and baptized"*). Those are the reasons why Jesus nor Nicodemus mentioned baptism in their entire discussion. Jesus also helps us understand the term of being 'Born Again' through conversion and humility: (*Matt. 18:3 "And said, Verily, I say unto you, 'Except a man be converted and become as little children, ye shall not enter the kingdom of heaven"*).

The born of *'water'* Jesus was explaining to Nicodemus was *'living water'*. This same *'living water'* is mentioned in *John 4:10 & 6:35*, which *John 7:38-39* explains its meaning the clearest: (*"He that believeth on me, as the scripture hath said, out of his belly shall flow rivers of 'living water'." "But this spake he of the Spirit, which they that believe on him should receive . . ."*). Jesus is using the term *'water'* as a representative of life. In order to sustain life you must include water. The same is true with the Spirit: *"And be born of the Spirit . . ."* (*Romas 8:10 ". . . the Spirit is life because of righteousness"*)

++ So the real question at hand is *how* do we become **'Born Again'** in Jesus' terms? It starts with our belief in Jesus as being the Son of God: (*1 John 5:1 "Whosoever believeth that Jesus is the Christ is born of God . . ."*), and then the new life that we live in obedience to the Father. This proves to be true because the rest of the conversation between Jesus and Nicodemus (*John 3:13-21*) will mainly pertain to the necessity of one's belief in Jesus in order to receive everlasting life. Even the 'light' that is mentioned in *John 3:19* pertains to Jesus (*John 9:5 ". . . I am the light of the world"*). What we 'believe' about Jesus opens the birth canal for us to receive the Spirit of righteousness, who identifies us to be 'born' of God: (*Romans 8:15-16 ". . . but ye have received the Spirit of adoption, whereby we cry, Abba, Father." "The Spirit itself bearth witness with our spirit, that we are the children of God"*).

On the flipside of this entire conversation concerning 'Born Again', one would normally place most of their attention on the 'babe' or 'new birth'.

But an equal factor that matters just as much with a new birth is who becomes their parent. When we hear news of a baby born into the family of a celebrity or icon, or into a family of royalty; for a moment we ogle over the cute, fat cheeks of the newest member. But it isn't very long before we shift our attention from who the baby is, to who the baby belongs to. We quickly acknowledge how blessed is the child, along with the many advantages it's going to have against the rest of the world simply because, not of who he is, but of who is his parent. And being 'Born Again' would not have any significant either without God becoming our Father as well. Other than becoming a new creature, (*2 Cor 5:17 "Therefore if any man be in Christ, he is a new creature . . ."*), **what else does it mean to become 'Born Again'**? Since Jesus says a person must be 'born again', this would imply that one would already have an existing parent. And if the first birth is not good enough, the first parent must be lacking certain qualities also to God. Jesus argued the difference to the Jews about having God as your father versus having the devil, (*John 8:38 "I speak that which I have seen with my Father: and ye do that which ye have seen with your father" 8:43-44 "Why do* *ye not understand my speech? even because ye cannot hear my word"* **"Ye are of your father the devil."** *8:47 "He that is of God hearth God's words, ye therefore hear them not, because ye are not of God.").* 1 John elaborates also on this parenthood with an illustration in the epistle: *1 John 3:9 "Whoever is born of God doth not commit sin; for his seed remaineth in him: and he cannot sin, because he is born of God" 3:10* **"In this the children of God are manifest, and the children of the devil***: whoever doth not righteousness is not of God . . ."*

Besides being adopted by God the Father and being able to enter into his kingdom, God does something else supernatural that we can feel the results soon afterwards when we're born again: (*Ezekiel 36:26-27 "A new heart also I will give you, and I will put a new spirit within you; I will take the stony heart out of your flesh, and I will give you a heart of flesh" "And I will put my spirit within you,* **and cause you to walk in my statutes, and ye shall keep my judgments, and do them***").* This is what Jesus was explaining to Nicodemus in *John 3:8* when he used directions and effects of the wind compared to the likeness of someone born of the *Spirit*. In other words, even though we may not know fully or understand exactly the spiritual mystery involved with transforming an individual into a Christian, our limited awareness does not prevent us from experiencing the effects. You do not see the wind blowing, but you do see the trees moving from its involvement.

What is the Primary Goal of a Christian

Whether it is a question that comes from one Christian to another Christian, or a question that comes from one sinner to a Christian about their main objective for being a *believer*, the most popular answers taught in churches today are: "to make it into heaven," "evangelism," and of course, "to love." Even though all of these teachings are true, they are only branches recorded in the Bible that connect to the root of our real assignment as being Christians. Many Christians live very confident each day with the idea that they're fulfilling God's desire for creating them when they aim at one of the above targets.

Did God create and assign us to *'evangelism'* as the primary goal once becoming Christians? Yes and No. *Yes*, he created and assigned us to evangelism because we are the 'salt' and the 'light' of the world: (*Matt. 5:13 "Ye are the salt of the earth . . ." 5:14 "Ye are the light of the world . . ."*). God knows non-Christians are going to critique our attitudes and behaviors long before they study or pick up a Bible. And we should also evangelize because Jesus commands us through the pattern of the Apostles to spread the gospel: (*Mark 16:15 ". . . Go ye into all the world, and preach the gospel to every creature"*). Through evangelism we carry knowledge and opportunity to a sinner as well as being available on their terms. Evangelism is by far the most effective method to reach a sinner concerning the gospel. And, *no*, God did not create and assign us to evangelism when we are not rightfully dividing the word: (*2 Timothy 2:15 ". . . a workman that needeth not to be ashamed, rightfully dividing the word of truth"*). I don't care how many doors you knock upon, or how many bystanders you approach; if you are not administering the 'word' correctly, evangelism promotes more harm than good: (*Luke 11:23 "He that is not with me is against me: and he that gathereth not with me scattered"*). So we must really examine our message before implementing evangelism as our primary goal. Apart from making mistakes in your doctrine that can quickly label you as a false teacher, bad theology creates more resistance toward the gospel than attraction.

Did God create and assign us to '*love*' as our primary goal once becoming Christians? Again, Yes and No. *Yes*, he created and assigned us to love because he loved us first, and because Jesus commands us to love each other: (*John 13:34 "A new commandment I give unto you, 'That ye love one another . . .'"*). And, *no*, God did not create and assign us to love in the manner that we often do when we express our intimate feelings to the ones who mean the most to us. This kind of love is based on conditions and is hardly the love *Paul* illustrates in Corinthians: (*1 Cor. 13:4-8 "Love suffereth long, and is kind; love envieth not; love vaunteth not itself, it is not puffed up" "Does not behave itself unseemly, seeketh not her own, is not easily provoked, thinketh no evil" "Rejoiceth not iniquity, but rejoiceth in the truth;" "Bearth all things, believeth all things, hopeth all things, endureth all things" "Love never faileth . . ."*) Jesus fulfilled each characteristic of real love for over 33 years on earth. How many times have we had the same opportunities since we've become Christians, and yet, not held our obligations? Most Christians won't represent the 'love' God is describing as their primary goal until they are at the end of life.

Did God create and assign us to '*make it into heaven*' as the primary goal once becoming Christians? Same answer: Yes and No. *Yes*, God did create and assign us to make it into heaven as the primary goal once becoming Christians because it's one of the 'high callings' of God: (*Philippians 3:14*). Also, we are to make it into heaven because Jesus wants us there: (*John 3:3 "And if I go and a prepare a place for you, I will come again, and receive you unto myself; that where I am, there ye may be also" John 17:24 "Father, I will that they also, whom thou hast given me, be with me where I am; that they may behold my glory . . ."*). And again, *no*, God did not create and assign us to make it into heaven as our primary goal once becoming Christians: if only to receive the amenities. Serving God to only reap good things and avoid the bad ones is the exact accusation Satan used against Job: (*Job 1:8-9 "And the Lord said unto Satan, 'Hast thou considered my servant Job . . .?'"* *"Then Satan answered the Lord, and said, 'Doth Job fear God for nought?'"*). "To make it into heaven" as the primary goal sounds like we don't necessarily care if we see God, as long as we're getting through the gates. Although there are many Christians wanting to go to heaven merely to escape hell, this superficial reasoning should only serve as an appetizer until you get the real meat for desiring an eternity in heaven.

++ Then what is the primary goal for a Christian if it is not *"to make it into heaven,"* *"evangelism,"* or *"to love?"*

It is to *"**Glorify the Father**."* God created and assigned us to glorify him: (*Isaiah 43:7 "Even every one that is called by my name: for I have created him for my glory . . ."*). The earlier goals are incentives and fruits that are attached to the primary root goal of glorifying the Father: (*John 15:8 "Herein is my Father glorified, that ye bear much fruit . . ."*). Whether it is through hope or work, it's all aimed at glorifying the Father, which results in others glorifying him as well: (*Matt. 5:16 "Let your light so shine before men, that they may see your good works, and glorify your Father which is in heaven"*). During one of Jesus' final prayers to the Father before his crucifixion, he mentions his achievement of glorifying God: (*John 17:4 "I have glorified thee on earth . . ."*). Do not make the mistake of overlooking this scriptural agenda by the distractions of a more popular obligation. God speaks quite candidly in the Bible about us glorifying him: (*Psalm 115:1 "Not unto us, O Lord, not unto us, but unto thy name give glory . . ."*). And the writer in Ecclesiastes, after completing the entire book, concludes that glorying God is the purpose of our existence: (*Ecc. 12:13 "Let us hear the conclusion of the whole matter: 'Fear God, and keep his commandments: for this is the whole duty of man'"*). Even hundreds of years later, *Paul* still places emphasis on this obligation that the Ecclesiastes writer concluded: (*1 Cor.6:20 "For ye are bought with a price, therefore glorify God in your body, and in your spirit, which are God's"*). On that note; all of us have disappointed and failed God as the Bible reveals: (*Romans 3:23 "For all have sinned, and come short of the glory of God . . ."*). This commandment to glorify God is a tremendous measuring rod that will extend all the way to the Judgment Seat, *"so they are without excuse."* (*Romans 1:21 "Because that, when they knew God, they glorified him not as God . . ."* *"1:28 "And even as they did not retain God in their* *knowledge, God gave them over to a reprobate mind, to do those things which are not convenient . . ." "1:32 "Who knowing the judgment of God, that they which commit such things are worthy of death . . .").* One revelation that should be obvious to every Christian is that even once we *make to into heaven,* after all that *evangelizing,* along with the sincere *love* we've shown, we are still going to do things throughout eternity that will ultimately **Glorify the Father**. So the next time we attempt to enlighten another Christian or sinner about our primary goal, let us start with the root instead of the fruit. This way we will have first gotten to the core or purpose of our relationship with God before campaigning the incentives and methods.

Final Thoughts

I hope by the time you reach this section of my book we will have became better friends, since we do share the same interest in pleasing our Lord. And although I know perhaps you did not agree 100% with some of my views and explanations, I trust that it has still been a thought-provoking experience.

I appreciate your concerns, sponsorship, and relinquished time taken for you to read this material, and I hope my book is successful in getting you to dig deeper in your quest to understand and complete the 'word' of God. Or for the most part, at least re-evaluate some doctrinal teachings you've acquired in an effort to know the truth about what really matters when glorifying God.

Also, part of my desire for the reader is that he/she be inspired toward studying the Scriptures with a sincere motive of finding and understanding the real truth behind God's love, purpose, and reward for mankind. I wouldn't want any reader to curse my interpretations, blow their top, and abuse pages in the Bible in an attempt to locate passages that might refute views expressed in this material.

Can a person find biblical passages that may help contradict some of my teachings? Of course, especially when they are taken out of context. If a person really wanted to be that 'technical' with one passage contradicting another in the Bible, two are in plain sight even during Jesus' ministry: (*Matt. 10:34 "Think not that I am come to send peace on earth: I came not to send peace . . ."*). Yet, in another verse Jesus proclaims a totally different agenda: (*John 14:27 "Peace I leave with you, my peace I give unto you . . .").* So if taken out of context, Christians can manifest legitimate arguments that will usually support their claim. For the readers who assert that Jesus did not have anything to do with peace descending upon earth; the passage does exist. For the readers who assert that Jesus was the ultimate giver and symbol of peace; the passage exists for them, too.

Other biblical passages that some claim contradict themselves during the recording of Jesus' ministry are: (*John 15:17 "These things I command you, that ye love one another . . ." 15:12 "This is my commandment, 'That ye love one another' . . .").* Still, we read a different expression being spoken in another verse by Jesus: (*Luke 14:26 "If any man come to me, and hate not his father, and mother, and wife, and children, and brethren, and sister, yea, and his own life also, he cannot be my disciple").* Although both readers can produce advocating passages to justify their assertions, the correct meanings will only be discovered when a study is performed with the help of a spiritually-discerning individual.

So for the offended critic of this book, save yourself the aggravation of high blood pressure, bad attitudes, and misled agendas aimed towards this material. Don't think I just woke up one morning, decided to write a book surrounding these specific topics, and raced to my computer. Before one word was typed, great consideration was taken concerning ethics, doctrines, and conflicting interpretations. I knew the topics were sensitive beliefs for my Christian brothers and sisters, and that's why I prayed earnestly before every session of documenting the words I share.

In fact, this book caught me way off-guard. Before I began writing it, I was heavily involved with the marketing of my 4th movie script: "The Search for Santa." And since this was a seasonal film, it was imperative that I put all my opportunity, experience, and effort through the small window *Christmas* allows before shutting it again. (Kind of like *Valentine's Day;* when the candy and flower businesses cram everything through the February 14th window before it closes.)

Anyway—all of my attention surrounded, at that time, the marketing of "The Search for Santa," barely leaving me with privileges for anything else. But for nearly two years I made time 5 to 6 days a week, almost every morning, to read and study my Bible for an uninterrupted average of 45 minutes. And before I studied, I prayed that God would give me his meaning of what I was reading, not my interpretation nor anyone else's. I wanted his true meaning of the way I was supposed to understand his word at the age and circumstance I was experiencing, right then. Having breakfast with God while studying his word and then marketing my movie script was the pinnacle of each blessed day for me. I was in ecstasy.

Even though I heard sermons preached and lessons taught which did not 'rightfully divide' the word or just plain missed the mark all together, it didn't irritate me as badly with some doctrinal teachings as it did with others. And, yes, although I did ponder the teachings, I never thought of storing them with the intention of writing a book.

Then it hit me. Instead of stacking my 'Good News Bible' and 'King James Bible' on top of each other, eating my breakfast, and reading them together as cross references, this was the day that everything would change. I carried the Bibles into the computer room and sat them close beside me. I thought, "This is strange. Not only is my morning routine being abruptly altered, but my desire to market my movie script has lost its zeal, too." I no longer had interest in promoting something that was so personal and dear to me for nearly three years. All of a sudden that craving vanished and was replaced by an obsession to write the book you've now read.

Although I was familiar previously with most of the book's interpretations, some of the revelations I expressed did not come to me until the actual writing of the material. I received and understood biblical mysteries for the very first time, only during writing this book. So as Christians, let's not get caught up in scholarly debates and signs-of-the-times. It's bad enough the Middle East has their ongoing Holy War; so are we creating a Church War? Have we forgotten the number one behavior that is supposed to identify us as being Jesus' disciples? That's right—through love, not through some traditional church rivalry. By love, and love alone are we to be recognized as Jesus' disciples. (*John 13:35 "By this shall all men know that ye are my disciples, if ye have love one to another."*)

It's very disappointing to discover that all churches are not concerned about the effect this 'disease' has on unbelievers and lukewarm Christians when they constantly judge and talk negatively about each other. *Paul* speaks specifically about this attitude: (*Romans 14:4 "Who art thou that judgest another man's servant? To his own master he standeth or falleth . . ."*). *Paul* evens corrects us in the matters of judging other church institutions as well: (*1 Cor. 5:12 "For what have I to do to judge them also that are without? Do not ye judge them that are within?" 5:13 "But them that are without God judgeth . . ."*). Non-Christians are already skeptical enough without their witnessing Christians slandering other Christians. Even when I entered a large print shop the service attendant agreed this was a book that needed to be written, because she heard church members saying terrible things about other members from different affiliations. Her job was only to stand there while the material was being printed. They were complete strangers who had nothing in common except for the copy machine. We should be ashamed to boasts the idea that we are ambassadors of Christ, yet sling mud at every opportunity into our spiritual brothers' faces.

I am not at all attempting to advocate one unified religion around the globe, but I am trying to motivate every Christian to accept his responsibility to hold the 'faith' together and be prepared at the end of time to give an account of his actions. (*Roman 2:6 "Who will render to every man according to his deeds" 2 Corinthians 5:10 "For we must all appear before the judgment seat of Christ; that everyone may receive the things done in his body, according to that he hath done . . ."*) Notice the passage does not say, "According to what others have done."

Unfortunately, that's how many Christians tend to judge themselves as being justified and righteous—based on the negative actions of others. But we read two illustrations that discard those excuses: (*Luke 18:11 "The Pharisee stood and prayed thus with himself, 'God, I thank thee, that I am not as other men are . . ." Galatians 6:4 "But let every man prove his own work, and then shall he have rejoicing in himself alone, and not in another"*). God hates this cheap way of Christians trying to exalt themselves by condemning others. If any Christian is going to use someone's life and behavior as a standard to measure the success of their spiritual agility, then they have the ultimate example in Jesus. See how you compare to Him.

We have a responsibility toward God, Jesus, and man to exhibit a Christian conduct that promotes love, unity, and peace above all other characteristics. Unfortunately, many of us have replaced godly personalities with ungodly ones. We've done this by judging, condemning and slandering everything we could about our neighboring congregations, pulpit predecessors, and ordinary Christians. One Christian attacking another Christian's theological belief and place-of-worship will have very little impact on him, especially if he's firm in his faith. But it may have a lot more impact on the offensive Christian during the Judgment.

Plus, let's not forget that when we're being judged and receive our 'reward' for the things we've done in this body, a large portion of our criticism will come from the position we were in, as well as the amount of time we spent doing it. For example—if you were married for an 'X' amount of days or years; the way you treated your spouse is going to have an enormous impact on your reward: (*Ephesians 5:22 "Wives submit yourselves to your own husbands . . ." 5:25 "Husbands, love your wives, even as Christ so loved the church . . ."*). If you were a parent of one, two, or five children; the way you raised those kids is going to have an enormous impact on your reward: (*Ephesians 6:4 "And ye fathers, provoke not your children to wrath: but bring them up in the nurture and admonition of the Lord"*). If you were rich; the way you trusted in your possessions is going to have an enormous impact on your reward at the end of time: (*Mark 10:24 ". . . But Jesus answered again . . . 'Children, how hard it is for them that trust in riches to enter into the kingdom of God'"*).

In case you want to know how I arrived at those conclusions. It's because when you examine the 4 Gospels in the New Testament, you can find several scenarios where Jesus uses a parable or actual situation to preach that people are going to be judged based on their position as well as their deeds. One illustration or example involved is the 'rich man.' (*Mark 10:21 ". . . 'One thing thou lackest . . .'"*) Although the rich man professed his obedience to God through following the Ten Commandments, his position of being rich held the final say-so in receiving full credit from Jesus.

Look at how teachers of the Law are going to be judged according to the Bible: (*James 3:1 "My brethren, be not many masters, knowing that we shall receive the greater condemnation"*). Even slaves will be critiqued on their positions, too: (*Titus 2:9 "Exhort servants to be obedient unto their own masters, and to please them well in all things . . ."*). What I'm trying to get the reader to understand is, **as Christians,** we are going to be severely critiqued as a people charged by God to love one another.

There won't be any support for ungodly attitudes and behaviors once we get to heaven concerning Christian unity. The Bible speaks clearly against participating or advocating any activity that wills itself above the will of God. Although many of us have a genuine, sincere motive to protect the truth and combat false doctrine, sometimes our methods of doing so are equally satanic. In this case, the end does not justify the means. There has to be another way to effectively teach and spread the Gospel besides exalting ourselves and condemning others. This Pharisees mentality of *"we know the Law and you don't"* and *"touch me not, for I am holier than thou,"* serves only as a deception to whoever admires it. God judges the "slander" to be equal in corruption: (*Jeremiah 6:28 ". . . walking with slanders . . . they are all corrupters" 9:4 ". . . and trust not in any brother: for every brother will utterly supplant, and every neighbor will walk with slanders"*).

The New Testament is filled with scriptures that forbid disciples from administering worldly passions toward any person, let alone against our brothers and sisters in the *faith.* For I know out of ignorance we utilized those behaviors in the past, but now there's no room or time for us to still attempt to capitalize on such selfishness: (*2 Timothy 2:19 ". . . Let everyone that nameth the name of Christ depart from iniquity" Titus 3:2 "To speak evil of no man, to be no brawlers, but gentle, showing meekness unto all men" James 2:8 ". . . thou shalt love thy neighbour as thyself, ye do well" 1 John 4:20 ". . . for he that loveth not his brother whom he hath seen, how can he love God whom he hath not seen" Luke 6:31 "And as ye would that men should do to you, do ye also to them likewise" James 4:11 "Speak not evil one of another, brethren. He that speaketh evil of his brother, and judgeth his brother, speaketh evil of the law, and judgeth the law . . ." Luke 6:37 "Judge not, and ye shall not be judged: condemn not, and ye shall not be condemned."*). Must I go on?

Isn't it ironic how most Christians will quickly admit, that if they had been back in the days when believers had such strong evidence and opportunity to absorb the prophesies and authentic teachings communicated, they would not have been foolish like the people of that time? Well, I hope our great, great grandchildren don't have the chance to label Christians of this era the same way. Are we blowing our opportunity also by nourishing a pride that feeds on making me *right* and you *wrong*, instead of humbly acknowledging God's grace?

Do you not recall the words Jesus said to the Pharisees and scribes concerning the final judgment? (*Matt. 12:41 "The men of Nineveh shall rise in judgment with this generation, and shall condemn it . . ." 12:42 "The queen of the south shall rise up in the judgment with this generation, and shall condemn it . . ."*) Jesus is warning us that there could be Christians from different church affiliations, the ones we've denounced and slandered, who might rise up in the judgment against this generation and possess the opportunity to condemn us, also.

Imagine denominational Christians having a part in judging non-denominational Christians. Or non-denominational Christians playing a role in judging denominational Christians? These are the scenarios we need to remember the next time we yearn to inflict wounds on neighboring Christians and continue spreading the disease that plagues our religious community.

Even though God created mankind in his image and equipped us with many capabilities, there are two endeavors he specifically asked us to leave to him. **'Vengeance'**: (*Romans 12:19 ". . . for it is written, 'Vengeance is mine; I will repay, saith the Lord'"*), and **'Judgment'** (*Psalms 75:7 "But God is the judge: he putteth down one, and setteth up another" Psalms 62:12 "Also unto thee, O Lord, belongeth mercy: for thou renderest to every man according to his work"*).

What a relief it is to know that the person who has judged and condemned my work does not have a heaven or hell in which to cast me. Since I do not agree with every doctrinal interpretation non-denominational and denominational institutions teach, I can only profess myself to be a God-fearing, Jesus-following, baptized, love-my-neighbor, Christian. I'm just like any other believer with the hope of spending eternity with

Jesus and escape the wrath to come on those who choose to deny God's will.

But while making this spiritual journey, one thing we all must be careful about is portraying ourselves like we've already received the prize. Even *Paul* speaks cautiously concerning this attitude: (*Philippians 3:12 "Not as though I had already attained, either were already perfect . . ." 3:13 "Brethren, I count not myself to have apprehended . . ."*). We all still need today for God to forgive our sins through his Son, no matter who we are.

I desire that you got as much out of reading this book as I did out of writing it. With so many books out there that promote strife and division, I'm excited to be a part of the program that employs a meek approach in representing Christianity. Disagreement, division and different beliefs were taken to the extreme during the 'Civil Rights' and 'Holocaust' eras. Remember how both of those events ended, and how a little leaven made the whole lump go bad? *"Blessed are the peace makers . . ."*

If for any reason you feel the urge to contact me concerning the views expressed in this material, email ***edmondsonanthony@yahoo.com***. I will respond to you as quickly and discreetly as possible.

May the God of grace grant you the pleasurable experience of choosing **love** over animosity, **peace** over strife, and **mercy** over judgment; while we wait together to hear those immaculate words spoken by Jesus, "Well done, thou good and faithful servant."